Spookiest Battlefields

Terrance Zepke

SPOOKIEST BATTLEFIELDS

ISBN-10: 0996065075

ISBN-13: 978-0-9960650-7-8

Cover design by Sara Whitford.

Safari Publishing

Inquiries should be addressed to: www.safaripublishing.net
For more about the author: www.terrancezepke.com

1. Ghosts-America. 2. Haunted Battlefields-America. 3. Paranormal-America. 4. Civil War. 5. Colonial America. 6. Military. 7. National Parks-America. 8. Famous Battles-American History. 9. Revolutionary War. I. Title.

Second Edition

Printed in the U.S.A.

Spookiest Battlefields

About the Author

Terrance Zepke has lived and traveled all over the world during her career as a travel writer. She has been to every continent and enjoyed all kinds of adventures—from dog-sledding in the Arctic to investigating haunted places ranging from lunatic asylums to lighthouses. She grew up in the South Carolina Lowcountry, which is full of haunted places and "haints." Terrance has a bachelor's degree in Journalism and a master's degree in Mass Communications from USC. She studied parapsychology at the renowned Rhine Research Center. She has written more than two dozen books about her favorite topics—ghosts and travel. See the back of this book for a complete list of her titles and you can also find out more about this author and her books at www.terrancezepke.com and www.terrancetalkstravel.com

"You don't have to believe in ghosts to realize that certain places in our national history are haunted with legends and spirits of long ago...Terrance is one of the most schooled experts on paranormal in the United States."
–Rick Steves, author, television & radio host

Introduction

Ever since I can remember, I've been fascinated by anything "haunted," "scary," "spooky," "creepy," or anything that is just plain "strange" or "enigmatic." I love poking around old historic sites, haunted houses (or anything that is reportedly haunted), and cemeteries.

I grew up in the South Carolina Lowcountry, so that helps explain my interest. The Lowcountry is all about Lowcountry Voodoo (Hoodoo), cemetery tours, and "haints" like Boo Hags and Bugaloos. My great aunts used to tell me the best ghost stories. I never tired of hearing about old plantations, lighthouses, and forts that were haunted by the likes of Civil War soldiers, lighthouse keepers, and spirits seeking lost love or retribution.

Eventually, my interest led me to participate in ghost investigations and to research paranormal activity. I began writing about it, too. I have written twenty-six books, many of them pertaining to the paranormal. This is the second book in my "spookiest" series. I'm a history buff, so I really enjoyed exploring these historic battlefields, learning about these momentous battles, and discovering the spirits that still linger in these places, perhaps still searching for a different outcome to their tragic deaths.

In addition to learning all about the ghosts of these battlefields, you'll also learn a lot about some of the most notable battles—and most defining moments—in American history from the War of 1812 to the Civil War. However, this book is not meant to be used as a historical and/or military reference. I have explained the basic facts of these battles because these facts have a significant correlation to battlefield hauntings. But the main purpose of this book is to detail paranormal activity and provide visitor information.

However, you will learn lots of interesting information, such as why no battle was ever fought at Valley Forge, yet it played a hugely significant role in the Revolutionary War. You'll learn the truth about General Robert E. Lee's surrender at Appomattox. The events of that day are quite extraordinary.

The most famous clashes in American history have taken place on the battlefields discussed in this reference. From Antietam National Battlefield to Wilderness Battlefield men fought valiantly but many were mortally wounded. Thousands of men died during these conflicts or from injuries suffered during these skirmishes. These were young men, many not even twenty years old, who surrendered their lives—not for fame or glory, but for freedom.

So, it's no wonder these places are among the most haunted in our great nation. The restless spirits of men who died on these fields can still be heard screaming in anguish or calling out battle commands. Other sounds of battle, such as drums beating and cannons firing, have been reported. Witnesses have seen campfires and phantom soldiers roaming the old battlefields. Read on to learn more about Old Green Eyes, Lady in White, Phantom Rider, an eerie fog, the Blue Light, hauntings at Devil's Den, Bloody Lane, Slaughter Pen, and much more...

Bivouac of the Dead

The muffled drum's sad roll has beat
The soldier's last Tattoo;
No more on life's parade shall meet
That brave and fallen few.
No vision of the morrow's strife
The warrior's dream alarms;
No braying horn, nor screaming fife,
At dawn shall call to arms.
Rest on, embalmed and sainted dead,
Dear as the blood ye gave,
No impious footstep here shall tread
The herbage of your grave.

—Poem by Theodore O'Hara

FYI: The biggest battle fought on American soil was the American Civil War.

Top Confederate leaders and commanders: Jefferson Davis, Robert E. Lee, Joseph E. Johnston, Stonewall Jackson, and Raphael Semmes.

Top Union leaders and commanders: Abraham Lincoln, Ulysses S. Grant, William T. Sherman, George B. McClellan, and David Farragot.

The Civil War was fought in twenty-three states over the course of four years. It began on April 12, 1861 when the first shot was fired at Fort Sumter, South Carolina. Lee surrendered to Grant at Appomattox Court House, Virginia on April 9, 1865.

It is estimated that 620,000–750,000 lives were lost during this war.

For a complete list of battles and specifics, such as locations and summaries, visit en.wikipedia.org/wiki/List_of_American_Civil_War_b attles

Vicksburg National Military Park

Vicksburg National Military Park

Location: Vicksburg, Mississippi

Established: February 21, 1899

Visitor Information

The park is open daily year-round, except on Thanksgiving, Christmas Day, and New Year's Day. There is a visitor's center and museum. An orientation film is shown in the visitor's center, which is the best starting point for your independent tour. The NPS estimates that it will take 2–4 hours to tour the park, which includes a 16-mile tour road, a restored Union gunboat, National Cemetery, twenty miles of trenches and earthworks, two antebellum houses, 144 emplaced cannons, and 1,325 monuments and markers. Additionally, the remains of Grant's Canal (the site where the Union Army tried to build a canal so they could avoid enemy fire) is located in Delta, Louisiana.

This 1,800-acre battlefield park was established by the federal government, which meant that they paid for all of the Union monuments, but the Confederate states didn't receive federal funding. So, they had to raise the funds over the course of many years. Some find this ironic given that the park is in a southern state.

Entrance fees are based on the number of people in a vehicle. Golden Age Passports (only available for those 62 years old and up), Vicksburg Annual Park Pass, and Annual Parks Passes are accepted. More than one million visitors come to Vicksburg National Military Park every year.

FYI: Ghost investigations are permitted here, but advance permission must be obtained through the National Park Service at Vicksburg National Military Park.

Vicksburg National Military Park
3201 Clay Street
Vicksburg, Mississippi 39183

www.nps.gov/vick/

Siege of Vicksburg by Kurz and Allison

About the Haunted Battlefield

The Battle of Vicksburg lasted forty-seven days. It took place from May 18 to July 4, 1863. This was perhaps the biggest showdown—or at least one of the most important—of the war.

Major General Ulysses S. Grant defeated Confederate Lt. General John Pemberton on the heels of General Robert E. Lee's devastating defeat at Gettysburg. Not only did this victory give the Union control of the Mississippi River, but also contributed greatly to the outcome of the war. Not only did this triumph yield the mighty Mississippi to the Union, but also resulted in disrupting communications between Confederate troops and the Trans-Mississippi Department for the remainder of the war.

Even though the Confederates held a perimeter around Vicksburg of sufficient gun pits, trenches, redoubts, and forts, Union forces managed to erect elaborate entrenchments behind these Confederate strongholds. So, despite their garrisons on Fort Hill, Fort Garrott, South Fort, Railroad Redoubt, and the Great Redoubt, the Confederates were now trapped. They were pinned in on one side by heavy gunfire from the Union fleet positioned on the Mississippi River and the trenches dug behind them by the Union forces, and more Union troops arrived to shore up their defensive line. The Union now had about 77,000 soldiers stationed in a circle around Vicksburg, cutting off almost all avenues of escape for the Confederates.

But this wasn't the only problem the Confederates were facing. There were rotting, stinking corpses of dead soldiers all over the area. Given this was summer in the south and we're talking about thousands of bodies, this was a serious issue for both sides. So much so, that a cease-fire was called so that both sides could bury their dead. During this time, it is reported that all the soldiers co-mingled as if they weren't in the middle of a war. It seems that both sides realized that in order to get the job done they would have to work side by side—war or no war.

But there was also the issue of disease. The townspeople and soldiers were battling illness, especially scurvy and dysentery. Some of the diseases were due to the conditions, but some were due to lack of food. There was precious little food, especially protein. Townspeople had to guard their meager food supplies from one another, as well as from soldiers from both sides.

Still another problem was safety. Properties were being damaged and destroyed due to heavy artillery fire. Housing was diminishing for townspeople and troops. Worse still, the people feared they might get hit in the crossfire. In order to avoid this, they came up with a creative solution. Roughly, 500 cave homes were created. Families moved themselves and some of their belongings into these caves in an effort to be comfortable and to save their most prized possessions, such as family portraits and heirlooms. Union troops dubbed the town "Prairie Dog Village" because the small caves resembled prairie dog dugouts—only larger and better furnished. Very few civilians died during this lengthy battle, which proved the cave homes were a good idea.

Lt. General John Pemberton

Lt. General John Pemberton ultimately had to admit defeat. His men were starving. He was low on ammunition and provisions. He had no way out and no hope to win. So, he sent a letter to Union General Ulysses S. Grant saying he would surrender but not unconditionally. His men must be allowed to go free. After some thought, General Grant agreed.

General Ulysses S. Grant

Grant agreed because he knew these men were no threat anymore. Their best fighting days were behind them. Sending them home sent the message of a defeated army. Also, he had no wish to feed and house 30,000 men or spend months trying to get them up north where they would have to be fed and tended to until after the war.

On July 4, 1863, Pemberton formally surrendered under an ancient town oak tree. Because this day was recognized as one of defeat and sorrow, Vicksburg did not celebrate the Fourth of July for many years thereafter. Some accounts indicate it wasn't celebrated until after World War II.

Confederate and Union soldiers were all buried here as it would have been too difficult to get all the bodies back to their respective home states.

USS Cairo

USS Cairo was a Union ship dispensed to destroy Confederate batteries and to rid the channel of underwater land mines. This ship was one of a small flotilla sent up the Yazoo River, due north of Vicksburg. Before it could reach its destination, it was struck by a naval mine. On December 12, 1862, it sank in less than fifteen minutes. Miraculously, there was no loss of life. What made this event significant is that it was the first ship in our history to be sunk by an electronically deployed torpedo, detonated by volunteers hidden behind the riverbank. Another interesting piece of trivia is that the ship was captained by Thomas Selfridge. He commanded three boats during this war, all three of which sank and all three had names beginning with the letter "C." Sailors are prone to believe in signs and be superstitious, so after this was realized, Selfridge was assigned to captain a ship beginning with the letter "O," the *USS Osage*. This ship survived without incident until the end of the war.

Arguably, Vicksburg is one of the most haunted battlefields in America. Some say it is second only to Gettysburg. Many have reported hearing cannons firing when there is no re-enactment taking place. Male shouts and cries have been heard, as well as moaning and groaning and gasping. Others have heard gunshots in the distance, but no logical explanation is ever discovered upon an investigation. But most disturbing of all is the soldiers who have been seen walking around the cemetery. Witnesses report seeing shadowy figures wearing what appears to be blue uniforms, so it is believed these are the spirits of Union soldiers. Questionable orbs and images have turned up in many photos.

Illinois Monument can be seen in the background. The monument has forty-seven steps to signify every day of the Vicksburg Battle.

Manassas National Battlefield Park

Manassas National Battlefield Park

Location: Manassas, Virginia

Established: October 15, 1966

Visitor Information

The park is 5,073 acres so be prepared to cover a lot of ground. The park and Henry Hill Visitor's Center, which includes a gift shop and museum, are open daily year-round except on Thanksgiving and Christmas Day. It closes at 5:00 p.m. but the grounds (including all trails and parking areas) are open until dusk. The Stone House is open on weekends only and closes at 4:00 p.m. Picnics and pets are permitted, but camping is not allowed. There is a campground just south of Manassas at Prince William Forest Park, which is a 10-minute drive.

Manassas National Battlefield Park
6511 Sudley Road
Manassas, VA 20109

www.nps.gov/mana

Manassas Battlefield gets more than 900,000 visitors annually. There are lots of different ways to explore this park and they are all free, but you must pay a fee to enter the park. There are ranger tours, a 45-minute film, a self-guided driving tour, the Brawner Farm Interpretive Center, and several trails, including Henry Hill, First Manassas, and Second Manassas Loop Trails. There is a phone tour option too. The Henry Hill Cell Phone Tour allows participants to use a downloadable map and their cell phones at designated stops to hear stories relating to these two battles. Call 703-253-9002 to access this tour option. This is the link for the map to accompany your phone tour:

www.nps.gov/mana/planyourvisit/upload/Cell-Phone-Tour-Bulletin-Final.pdf

There are different passes you can buy, such as the Manassas Annual Pass, Interagency Annual Pass, Senior Pass, Access Pass, and Military Pass. Other battlefield parks discussed in this reference that are located nearby include Antietam National Battlefield, Fredericksburg & Spotsylvania National Military Park, and Robert E. Lee Memorial.

About the Haunted Battlefield

Manassas National Park is the site of two Civil War Battles: First Battle of Bull Run and the Second Battle of Bull Run. The First Battle of Bull Run (also known as First Battle of Manassas) was fought on July 21, 1861. The Second Battle of Bull Run (also known as Second Battle of Manassas) took place from August 28–30, 1862.

For two hours, several regiments from both sides engaged in combat near Stone House. Tourists came by horse and buggy from Washington, DC to watch the First Battle of Bull Run. They sat on the sidelines enjoying picnics and cheering as if watching a ball game instead of a battle! It wasn't until after the First Battle of Bull Run that they took the situation seriously, finally realizing that this wasn't going to be a short war.

More than one thousand men were wounded during this intense conflict. This led to Union soldiers seizing the Stone House and converting it into a hospital. They hung white flags in the windows to let the enemy know it was a medical facility. This did not make it exempt from artillery fire. Confederate forces were relentless in their assault. Eventually, they took control of Stone House and kept control until March 1862.

Stone House

During the Second Battle of Bull Run, Stone House was again converted into a hospital. Once again, white flags were placed in the windows in the hopes the structure would not be attacked. And once again, Confederate soldiers ignored the signs. They were victorious and once again took control of Stone House.

Many men died inside this structure. Some died quickly while others lingered, slowly dying from battle wounds. A total of 9,000 men died during these two battles at Manassas. We don't know how many died on the battlefield and how many died in this hospital, but it's safe to assume that many of these soldiers died after being brought to the hospital. In fact, there are documented reports of the filth and stench inside the makeshift hospital as there was nothing to do with the mortally wounded while they were still coming under attack. Eventually, some were buried in the yard.

It is unknown if the owner, Henry Matthews, returned to this house after the war, which by that time must have surely been in bad condition. Some of the men had carved their names in the floorboards as they lay dying, presumably in hopes of being remembered.

With all this death and suffering, it is no surprise there are lingering spirits here. Some visitors have reported seeing strange orbs and shadowy figures in photos they have taken, especially at the Stone House.

Many claim they smelled gunpowder and felt the presence of soldiers in the woods. Some say they have seen shadowy figures among the trees and have heard male voices shouting *"Remember us!"*

Some visitors swear they hear a harmonica and men clapping, singing, and foot tapping. A few even say they have seen a cluster of men around a campfire and tents, as close as one hundred feet from the visitors. As they looked at the bluish figures that resembled Union soldiers, witnesses wondered if they might be war re-enactors or trespassers since they know that camping is forbidden in the park. They watched in amazement as everything went dark. The noisy group of men and their tents and campfire were nowhere to be seen or heard!

But what is most commonly reported and probably the most disturbing is the screams and cries. During this battle, General Robert E. Lee needed to get supplies to his men so he ordered a railroad to be built.

All the men assigned to this project were killed while working on the railroad. It is believed to be their dying screams and cries that visitors hear.

First Battle of Bull Run by Kurz and Allison

Historic sites in and around the battlefield:

Stone House (near the intersection of Sudley Road and Lee Highway)

Stone Bridge (north of Lee Highway at Fairfax-Prince William Company Line)

Brawner's Farm (off Pageland Lane at western end of the battlefield) is now a museum chronicling the Second Battle of Manassas.

Battery Heights (off Lee Highway)

Matthews Hill (off Sudley Road) where the first battle began

Unfinished railroad grade and Deep Cut (off Featherbed Lane)

Groveton (remains of Civil War village) and Confederate Cemetery (off Lee Highway)

Chinn Ridge is the site of major assault during the Second Battle of Bull Run.

Hazel Plain and Portici (plantation ruins).

Robinson House was the home of freed slave, James Robinson. The ruins of this home are on the Henry Hill

Loop Trail, which has informational plaques throughout the 1.1-mile trail.

FYI: Only one civilian was killed during the Battle of Bull Run. An old woman, Judith Carter Henry, who was bedridden, was killed by artillery fire. She is buried in her family's cemetery on Henry Hill.

Second Battle of Bull Run by Currier and Ives

Shiloh National Military Park

Shiloh National Military Park

Location: Shiloh, Tennessee

Established: December 27, 1894

Battle of Shiloh by Thure de Thulstrup

Visitor Information

The park is open during daylight hours every day throughout the year, except on Thanksgiving, Christmas Day and New Year's Day. There is a visitor's center and museum, which is called Corinth Civil War Interpretive Center. It features many Civil War exhibits. Additionally, there are a couple of visitor films, including *Shiloh: Fiery Battle*.

The 240-acre park can be explored in a variety of ways. The most popular option is a self-guided car tour, which is a 12.7-mile route with twenty stops, including Hornet's Nest and Peach Orchard. Visitors may buy a 75-minute audio CD tour in the park's bookstore to use during their self-guided car tour. Additionally, there are ranger tours and programs (including a junior ranger program for kids), re-enactments, and special events. The park may be explored on foot, as well.

The park is handicap-accessible. Dogs on leashes and bicycles are permitted in the park. Bikes must stay on paved roads and dogs are not allowed inside any of the buildings or in the cemetery. Camping is not allowed in Shiloh, but there are local campgrounds. Also, there are hotels in nearby Corinth, Mississippi, and Savannah, Tennessee. Information about these options can be obtained at Corinth Civil War Interpretive Center.

There is no fee to go into this visitor's center, but there is an admission fee for Shiloh National Military Park. This fee is waived if you have an Annual Park Pass, Golden Age Pass, National Park Pass, or Golden Access Pass.

1055 Pittsburg Landing Road

Shiloh, TN 38376

www.nps.gov/shil/

FYI: Shiloh Battlefield is about 150 miles from Stones River National Battlefield.

About the Haunted Battlefield

On April 6 and 7, 1862, the largest battle in the Mississippi Valley campaign occurred here. More than 23,000 lives were lost during this two-day conflict. This included 13,047 Union soldiers and 10,699 Confederate soldiers. The Army of Tennessee, Army of Ohio, and Army of Mississippi were all involved in this bloody battle, which ended in a Union victory.

At dawn on April 6, 1862, 40,000 Confederate soldiers attacked Federal forces at Pittsburgh Landing, which is on the Tennessee River, near Shiloh Church. After this battle, it became known as Shiloh Hill. Confederate General Johnston was killed during this skirmish. A bullet struck his right leg and he bled to death.

P.G.T. Beauregard became the first Confederate officer to be appointed a Brigadier General in the Provisional Army of the Confederate States on March 1, 1861. Beauregard had been positioned in the rear of the army during this battle. When Johnston was mortally wounded, he assumed command of the army. At nightfall, he gave the command for his men to cease fighting. Beauregard believed he had all but won this battle and could simply wrap it up in the morning. Before he got a chance to do anything, General Grant attacked at dawn's first light. During April 7, the fighting continued. Who knows how things would have turned out if the Army of Ohio hadn't arrived? But they did. These reinforcements provided the Union with even more men and weapons. The Confederates had little choice but to retreat to Corinth. This battle was over.

Beauregard's decision to stop fighting became one of the most controversial of the War Between the States. Many historians believe things might have turned out very differently if this battle had been won by the Confederacy. Despite this loss at Shiloh, Beauregard was promoted to full general—one of only seven appointed to this rank—a few months later. However, some of the decisions he made remain controversial, including taking medical leave without advance permission.

With all this bloodshed and death, it is easy to see why this battlefield is haunted. The most famous ghost at Shiloh is the "Drummer Boy." According to legend, on April 7, 1862 a Union officer ordered the drummer to play "Retreat" as Confederate soldiers approached. Contrary to his orders, the drummer played "Attack." So, of course, the soldiers attacked. Not only did they go on the offensive, they won. After the battle, the officer went looking for the drummer boy to thank him for his service. Even though the boy had disobeyed a command, the officer was willing to overlook his disobedience given the outcome. The officer discovered the drummer boy had died during this battle.

In 1940, road work was being done in this area. The crew found the skeleton of a child. He still had the remains of the drum cord around his neck. Many believe that the drum music and sighting of a shadowy figure that appears to be a very small soldier is the spirit of the "Drummer Boy." Others say they have seen what appears to be the soldiers' spirits walking around the field looking disoriented. Cannon fire has been heard on occasion. Some say they have gotten cold as soon as they entered the cemetery, even in the middle of summer. Could it be that soldiers' spirits are still here at Shiloh, still fighting in some desperate hope of changing their destiny?

Drummers played an important role in the war. Since it was nearly impossible for the soldiers to hear anything above the sounds of battle, officers relied on drummers to let their men know what to do.

There was a drumroll for every command from "meet here" to "retreat."

Drummers did double duty and their second job was just as important as their primary one. When they weren't "making announcements" they made sure that wounded soldiers got medical treatment. They carried injured soldiers from the field to the hospital.

FYI: Shiloh National Military Park is the third oldest battlefield in the National Park Service (NPS). The park looks pretty much the same as it did in 1862 as far as roads, fields, and woods. The only big difference is the undergrowth is much greater after all these years.

Brandywine Battlefield State Park

Brandywine Battlefield State Park

Washington's Headquarters

Location: Chadds Ford, Pennsylvania

Established: 1949

Visitor Information

Park hours vary throughout the year so check the website before visiting. The park is closed from December 29 to March 9, as well as most holidays. There is no fee to enter the park or to go in the visitor's center or to use public picnic areas and restrooms. However, there is a fee to tour the house, museum, and see the film. Discounted rates are given for children and seniors. Many special seasonal events and re-enactments are held each year in the fifty-acre park.

The visitor's center features artifacts, dioramas of battle scenes, and educational exhibits. There are two houses on site that can be toured: colonial-era Benjamin Ring House and the Gideon Gilpin House. The Benjamin Ring House was used as headquarters by George Washington while Marquis Lafayette stayed at the Gideon Gilpin Farmhouse. Both houses have been restored, including period furnishings. Additional outbuildings include a springhouse, carriage house, smokehouse, barn, and corn crib.

The Battle of Brandywine occurred at Birmingham Township—not in what is now the state park. This area is where the officers slept and served as their headquarters, but not the scene of the battle. There is at least one mass grave near Birmingham.

Brandywine Battlefield State Park is in southeastern Pennsylvania, about one mile east of Chadds Ford, PA on US 1.

1491 Baltimore Pike

Chadds Ford, PA 19317

A handy self-guided driving map can be found on
www.ushistory.org/brandywine/index.htm

brandywinebattlefield.org/

About the Haunted Battlefield

Brandywine was the site of one of the largest land battles of the Revolutionary War. Yet it was never intended to be a place of battle.

Due to poor reconnaissance, General Washington inadvertently got too close to his enemy, who had landed near Elkton, Maryland. General Howe, realizing Washington's blunder, began moving his troops into position to trap the American troops. His plan was to force Washington to move his troops towards the Delaware River, where they would then be trapped between Howe's Army and the Navy. The flanking maneuver executed by Howe is still studied in military history.

This gambit forced Washington to move inland—his only viable option. He was too shrewd to get pinned between the British army and navy. He knew that was a surefire defeat.

This epic battle took just one day—September 11, 1777. Despite Washington's best efforts, it was a British victory. This win helped to ensure their victory in Philadelphia, which was a crushing blow to the Continental Army. Philadelphia was the largest city of the thirteen colonies so this was a huge loss.

The British occupied Philadelphia from September 26, 1777 until June 1778. This resulted in a disruption in the supply line for the American troops, as well as the loss of eleven artillery pieces that were seized by the British.

There were 26,000 soldiers involved in this battle. The official British account is 587 casualties. However, we'll never know how many Americans sacrificed their lives for our independence as those figures have never been revealed. One British officer claimed that 400 American soldiers were buried by British soldiers. Another claimed 502 lay dead on the field at the end of that day. Howe's report to his superior stated 300 American men had been killed at the Battle of Brandywine. Major Nathaniel Greene estimated 1,200–1,300 men were killed that day.

There were many wounded and prisoners of war that day. Those numbers cannot be confirmed either. We do, however, know that Marquis de Lafayette was one of the many wounded at the Battle of Brandywine.

Marquis de Lafayette (Gilbert du Motier), 1791. Portrait by Joseph-Desire Court

FYI: The Marquis de Lafayette (1757–1834) served in the Continental Army during the American Revolutionary War. Lafayette fled his homeland during the French Revolution. He was a great leader and statesman, which is how he came to be known as the "Hero of Two Worlds."

The American Continental Army retreated at dusk to Chester City. They marched forty miles in two days following the Battle at Brandywine. It was five days before the British followed them. They had been left to treat the wounded and bury the dead.

General Wayne, 1794

On September 11, 1777 Wayne commanded the Pennsylvania Line at Brandywine. He was successful in holding the line against General Wilhelm von Knyphausen. General Anthony Wayne earned the nickname "Mad Anthony" after the Battle of Stony Point. Wayne dared to take nearly 1,400 men up the side of Stony Point in the middle of the night. This was a treacherous climb and his men were armed only with bayonets so as not to give any warning to British sentries. Silently, they scaled the walls of the fort and breached it. The battle was over in less than half an hour. Wayne lost only 15 men during this skirmish while the British lost 70 and another 550 were taken as prisoners of war. However, a Congressional medal and a nickname is not the end of the story.

It continues to this day. A phantom horseman has been seen crossing Chadds Ford and the Brandywine River ever since that battle. He only appears in the fall and only on nights when there is a full moon. He has been described by witnesses as wearing white knee pants, black boots, and a long blue coat with big brass buttons (like the uniform of the Continental Army). He carries a long sword and sits astride a big, pale mare.

When the phantom rider has been seen, it is in the Brandywine Valley galloping through the woods in a blaze of fury as if fleeing for his life—or fighting for it. At least that is how the scene has been described by those who have witnessed this spectacle.

There have also been sightings of the phantom rider along US 1 and Route 322, which you can imagine has shocked and baffled motorists. These witnesses swear the ghostly rider and horse seem to glow in the dark and pay no heed to them. I'm sure that the white horse and white knickers illuminated by the light of the full moon lend an eerie glow and create a memorable sight to all who witness the phantom rider and his horse.

But who is this mysterious ghostly figure? It is believed this spooky spectral is "Mad Anthony." Why he is frantically galloping across roads, rivers, and fields is anyone's guess. There has been plenty of speculation over the years, as well as hundreds of sightings. Perhaps he is still trying to reach Philadelphia to warn his men. Or maybe, he is desperately trying to change the outcome of this battle.

An even creepier explanation is that he is looking for his bones. He was disinterred in 1809 from Fort Presque Isle, Pennsylvania to the family cemetery in Radnor, Pennsylvania. His body was boiled to remove any remaining flesh. His bones were put into two large saddlebags and transported home by his son, Isaac Wayne, but many of these bones were lost along Route 322. According to legend, the ghost of Mad Anthony is still searching for his missing bones.

Wayne's defeat at Brandywine was the biggest blow to his career. During this showdown, he spent hours riding wildly across this area trying to rally his men. He fairly flew across this field shouting orders and words of encouragement to his men to *"Hold the line!"* and to *"Fight for freedom!"* He continued long after he must have known the futility and inevitable loss. General Wayne had been given strict orders from his Commander-in-Chief, General George Washington. Washington had been explicit that he was to hold Chadds Ford at all costs. It was critical to stop the advancing British from reaching Philadelphia.

Fortunately, the errors at Brandywine were among the precious few made by Washington during the American Revolution. We did win the war and sent the British packing. Thanks to his victory in winning our freedom from the Crown, America chose George Washington as our first president.

There has been so much paranormal activity reported at Brandywine that the Rhine Research Center investigated during the early 1980s. At that time, the parapsychology program was still part of North

Carolina's Duke University. Their investigation lasted twenty-four hours and included psychics, EVPs, and other standard research methods.

The psychics reported nine different entities at this battlefield, including one that resides in the house that once served as Washington's headquarters, inside the spring house, and in the old barn. Both the barn and spring house were used as holding cells for prisoners. The main house was used as a hospital.

It is believed that the ghost of the original owner of the house, who hung himself inside the house, is one of the lingering spirits. Other spirits that have been identified include an old man (in the spring house), a young girl in one of the bedrooms, a soldier in the back stairwell, and a couple of male spirits remain unidentified.

Recently, the farm was investigated by TAPS, which is the Atlantic Paranormal Society. They are more commonly known as *The Ghost Hunters* (SyFy Channel). Their findings were in line with those of the Rhine Research Center.

Nation Makers, **by Howard Pyle, is a famous painting featuring the Brandywine Battle. The significance of this battle was that the British were subsequently able to seize control of Philadelphia, which led to their victory at the Battle of Germantown.**

FYI: The Battle of Brandywine introduced important new developments in military technology and tactics, such as the Ferguson rifle. British Army officer, Captain Patrick Ferguson, invented the first breech-loading weapon in 1772, which was the first rapid fire rifle. It could fire six times a minute. Roughly, two hundred Ferguson rifles were made and used during the Battle of Brandywine. A working replica of this firearm is on exhibit at Brandywine Battlefield Park.

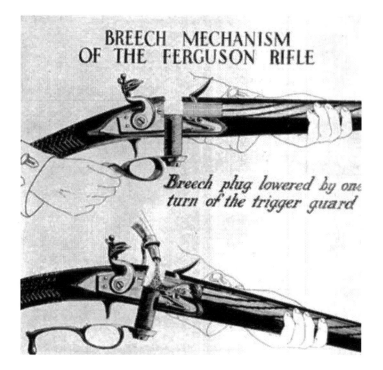

Stones River National Battlefield

Stones River National Battlefield

General Rosecrans (atop his horse) rallies his troops at Stones River. Painting was created by Kurz and Allison.

Location: Murfreesboro, Tennessee

Established: The cemetery was established in 1865, but it was 1927 before Congress authorized the establishment of this park. It was transferred from the US War Department to the National Park Service in 1933 and designated as a national battlefield in 1960.

Visitor Information

The park, which used to be much larger than what you see today, was placed on the National Register of Historic Places in 1966. Visitors can explore the park in a variety of ways. There are ranger programs and special events, including living history programs.

There is a trail through the woods that originates at the picnic area and extends to Stop #2 on the self-guided tour. Picnicking is only permitted in this designated area. There is also a 2.2-mile route along the tour road that can be enjoyed on foot or on a bicycle. No other recreational activities are permitted. Leashed pets are permitted everywhere except inside the visitor's center.

There is a visitor's center, bookstore, and museum. The visitor's center is handicap-accessible. The park is open daily throughout the year, except on Thanksgiving and Christmas Day. There is no admission fee.

FYI: The NPS does allow ghost investigations but a permit must be obtained. There is also a fee to have a ranger escort your group through the park since visitors cannot be on federal land after hours unless a government employee accompanies them.

Rutherford County Chamber of Commerce has a list of places to stay: www.rutherfordchamber.org

3501 Old Nashville Highway

Murfreesboro, TN 37129

www.nps.gov/stri/

The park is twenty-eight miles southeast of Nashville.

About Haunted Battlefield

This battle lasted for three days, from December 31, 1862 to January 2, 1863. By nightfall on December 30, the Union's Army of Cumberland and Confederate's Army of Tennessee were in place. Both leaders spent a great deal of the night plotting their strategies.

At daybreak on the last day of 1862, Confederate General Bragg attacked Union General Rosecrans and his troops. It looked as if General Bragg was going to win this battle until more Union troops arrived.

General Bragg

Desperate to play his last card, General Bragg sent some of his men on a deadly mission. He ordered them to take up a position on a hill where sharpshooters could pick off enemy troops, which was already well-guarded by Union sharpshooters. But in order to complete their mission, his men would have to march across an open field where they would most likely meet enemy fire—and that is precisely what happened. Bragg faced disciplinary action when some of his remaining troops complained to his superiors about his actions at Stones River. They wanted him relieved of his command.

Despite this being a small battle in the scheme of the war, Stones River Campaign resulted among the highest in respect of loss of lives for both sides. There was 2,800 dead and 15,000 wounded. The worst part is the Battle at Stones River was considered to be tactically inconclusive. Even though losses were heavy for both sides, it was a moral victory for the Union. The only thing that saved General Bragg's command is that the Confederacy was unable to find a suitable replacement in a hurry.

With all this death and despair, it is not surprising that ghostly activity has been reported. The most common complaint is that people feel like they're being followed.

The most paranormal activity has been reported at Slaughter Pen. Visitors complain of getting chilled and experiencing an overall eerie feeling.

Several ghost groups, including S.P.I.R.I.T. (Society for Paranormal Investigations & Research in Tennessee) have researched this area. Most conclude there are thousands of lingering spirits here. EVPs and orbs are often reported.

According to most folks who have investigated here, if you call for the ghosts, they will respond by interfering with your equipment. If you stop calling them, this interference stops. One group says that a campfire showed up in their images where there was no campfire! Apparitions have been seen on occasion too by both visitors and park service staff. Rangers have also reported hearing cannon fire, but they never found a reason for these sounds when they investigate.

Re-enactments are held periodically. Participants claim to have seen a soldier around a campfire, but the soldier and campfire disappear when they go closer to investigate. Park rangers have reported seeing a man who appears to be wearing some kind of uniform. When a ranger requests the man to stop and identify himself, he holds his arms in the air as if surrendering and then vanishes into the darkness. When the ranger pursues the mysterious figure, he finds nothing—no footprints or any other indication that someone was just there.

There have been sightings of a headless horseman, who is believed to be the lingering spirit of Lt. Colonel Garesche. This Cuban-American was a graduate of West Point and an officer in the Union's Cumberland Army. He served with distinction in the Mexican-American War but was killed during his first battle of the Civil War. It was on December 31, 1862 when he was riding with General Rosecrans toward Round Forest. His death was gruesome, his head blown off his body by a cannonball. Reportedly, his spooked horse kept riding and it was twenty or thirty yards before the body fell off the animal. His headless corpse is buried in Mt. Olive Cemetery in Washington, DC, but his spirit may still be roaming the area where he lost his life.

In addition to these bizarre sightings, witnesses have reported an eerie silence. In this wooded area, it is remarkable that there are times when the sound of the wind in the trees or leaves rustling or crickets chirping or hoot owls or tree frogs cannot be heard—only a peculiar silence except for the sounds of phantom footsteps.

General Rosecrans

FYI: There are 7,123 tombstones in the cemetery with 6,100 belonging to Union soldiers. There are more than 2,500 unknown graves believed to hold more than one body in each one. This may be another soldier or a member of the soldier's family as was often the case with post-Civil War burials. Roughly 1,300 Confederate soldiers are buried in Confederate Circle in Evergreen Cemetery. Originally, they were buried alongside Union soldiers. Later, they were moved to their own cemetery, which deteriorated to the point that the remains were moved to Evergreen Cemetery.

Pyne's Ground Plum & Tennessee coneflower

FYI: There is a dozen specially adapted species of plants, such as the Tennessee coneflower (right) and Pyne's Ground Plum (left) that can only be found in middle Tennessee, including the cedar glades at Stones River Battlefield.

Chickamauga & Chattanooga National Military Park

Chickamauga & Chattanooga National Military Park

Location: Fort Oglethorpe, Georgia and Lookout Mountain, Tennessee

Established: Chickamauga and Chattanooga National Military Park was officially established by the US War Department during September 1895. It was transferred to the NPS in 1933.

Visitor Information

The Chickamauga and Chattanooga National Military Park is open daily until sunset. Both visitor centers are open daily from 8:30 a.m. to 5:00 p.m. except on Christmas Day and New Year's Day. There are weekend tours of the Cravens House on Lookout Mountain. There are 1,400 monuments and historical markers on these battlefields. This was one of the first US military parks.

Chickamauga Battlefield offers a seven-mile self-guided driving tour that includes monuments, historical markers, and trails for hiking and horseback riding. The trails range from five to fourteen miles in length. Its visitor center has many fascinating exhibits, including the Fuller Gun Collection. There are no entrance fees.

3370 Lafayette Road, Fort Oglethorpe, GA 30742

Lookout Mountain Battlefield also offers visitors a self-guided tour complete with monuments, historical markers, trails, and the Cravens House. There is no fee to go inside the Cravens House, but there is a small fee (free for those 15 years old or younger) to go into Point Park at Lookout Mountain Battlefield.

110 Point Park Road, Lookout Mountain, TN 37350

www.nps.gov/chch

***Battle of Chickamauga* by Kurz and Allison**

About the Haunted Battlefield

Chickamauga is derived from an ancient Indian word meaning "River of Death." The Cherokee Indians settled in this area, which had become a large farming community by the mid-1800s.

This Battle of Chickamauga took place from September 18–20, 1863, although it was only a brief skirmish that occurred on September 18. The real battle took place on September 19 and 20 and resulted in the largest Confederate victory in the Western theater. The Confederates won this battle for several reasons.

Significantly, Federal troops weren't expecting to encounter Confederate troops. More importantly, Confederate troops outnumbered Union troops, which was a rare occurrence.

The Confederacy can also thank General Rosecrans for their victory. He ordered Brig. General Wood's regiment to move his men to fill a gap. Wood knew there was no gap but was afraid to argue with his superior. He had already been chastised twice during the war for questioning orders. Wood did as he was told, thus creating a hole in their line. Seeing this, the Confederates struck hard and fast. Rosecrans and his men were all forced to scatter and retreat.

But there is plenty of blame to go around. If Burnside had followed orders to leave Knoxville and join Rosecrans, then perhaps Rosecrans wouldn't have been forced to retreat.

General George H. Thomas earned the nickname "The Rock of Chickamauga" for his persistent defense of Horseshoe Ridge, an important defensive post. He grabbed retreating men and continued fighting until he received orders from Rosecrans to retreat. His suggestion that Rosecrans attack the next day was ignored by General Rosecrans, who stayed in Chattanooga. Thomas is considered to be one of the best generals to have served in the Union army.

Repeating rifles were introduced during this war and proved invaluable, especially at Horseshow Ridge and Alexander's Bridge.

A major tactical mistake for the Confederacy was Bragg's failure to go after Rosecrans. He most likely could have defeated him, which may have led to a different outcome for the Confederacy. Instead, Union troops ended up seizing control of Chattanooga, which made the loss of lives at Chickamauga all for naught. Bragg lost 20 percent of his men only to give up Chattanooga in the end.

But the biggest legacy may be "Old Green Eyes." According to legend, this is the ghost of a Confederate soldier who was beheaded by a cannonball. The sightings date back more than 150 years and are usually seen when it is foggy. Witnesses swear they will never forget the sight as long as they live. It is two glowing green eyes and the sound of a raspy voice groaning, unlike anything they've ever heard before. They report it as "human-like" but not human. Edward Tinney was a park historian and ranger for nearly 20 years. He gives an eerie description. He calls it a "thing" with long thin hair, greenish-orange eyes, and teeth that look like fangs. Park ranger, Charlie Fisher, claims cars have wrecked on occasion from being so spooked by the sight.

Some believe this spirit has been around since before the war. They think it is more likely the spirit of a Cherokee Indian than a Confederate soldier. This was Native American land, so it is possible. Others think it is a ghost panther. Spirits can assume the bodies of animals as easily as humans, according to some believers.

There have also been reports of a "Lady in White" who appears in a wedding gown. Who is she and why is she here? Some speculate that she is still searching for her fiancé who was one of the many lives lost during this bloody war.

A training camp was set up here during the Spanish-American War, which was fought in 1898. Many men died of disease while stationed here. It is possible they also haunt this place.

Many soldiers lay a long time before being buried while the Civil War raged on. Their corpses were hastily buried two or three months after their deaths in unmarked graves. Maybe they remain restless due to not getting a proper burial.

We may not know exactly who haunts this park or why, but we do know there have been thousands of reports of phantom horses' hooves, gunfire, men shouting and screaming, and the smell of ale. Some are spooked by the feeling of being watched. This is compounded by the sight of bushes blowing wildly on windless nights.

If you'd like to learn more about the Battle of Chattanooga, visit www.civilwar.org/battlefields/chattanooga.html

Terrance Zepke

Little Bighorn Battlefield National Monument

Little Bighorn Battlefield National Monument

Lithograph titled "The Custer Fight" by Charles Marion Russell.

Location: Crow Agency, Montana

Established: January 29, 1879

Visitor Information

Little Bighorn Battlefield National Monument is open year-round except on Thanksgiving, Christmas Day, and New Year's Day. Visitors can explore the battlefield, Indian Memorial, Deep Ravine Walking Trail, Custer National Cemetery, and visitor's center, which includes a museum, gift shop, and a 30-minute orientation film. Hours of operation and special events vary seasonally so check the website before you go. Visitors can opt to explore the park on their own, take a cell phone audio tour, or purchase the self-guided audio tour. More than 400,000 visitors come to this battlefield each year.

756 Battlefield Tour Road
Crow Agency, Montana 59022
www.nps.gov/libi

www.custermuseum.org

"The Whites Want War, And We Will Give It to Them."
—Sitting Bull

About the Haunted Battlefield

On June 25, 1875 war broke out between the Western Sioux Nation and the US Army. The American government was responsible because they repeatedly tried to force the Indians off their land and onto reservations. They broke treaty after treaty with them as the American population kept expanding westward. The latest treaty was violated when the government discovered gold in the Black Hills of North Dakota. Lakota Chiefs Sitting Bull and Crazy Horse had successfully avoided being subjugated onto reservations for more than ten years.

Custer (seated) and Bloody Knife (kneeling beside Custer) was Custer's favorite Indian Scout.

The US Army gave orders for all Indians in Montana to go to their reservations or face the consequences. Knowing that war was inevitable, Sitting Bull and Crazy Horse organized 10,000 men to fight for their cause. They gathered at a spot in southern Montana known as Little Big Horn.

The first troops arrived on June 17, 1875 and were quickly defeated by the Indians. The US Army was not prepared for such an organized counterattack. On June 22, 7th Cavalry of the US Army, led by Lt. Col. George Custer, arrived at Little Big Horn. He was immediately sent on a scouting mission. He soon learned that a large Indian village was situated in the Little Big Horn River valley. Hoping to gain the element of surprise, Custer attacked this village.

He thought he was in good shape with 600 men. Imagine his surprise when he encountered more than 10,000 Indian warriors! Not only was he outmanned, but the Indians had received fair warning, and so they had been able to fully prepare for the attack. Like the first troops, the 7th Cavalry was soon disposed of by the Indians. The Battle of the Little Bighorn did not end at Last Stand Hill as popularly believed but rather in Deep Ravine.

Many military experts say this defeat rests solely on Custer's arrogance. He blatantly ignored reports of a large Indian presence, steadfastly believing the numbers had been inflated. Furthermore, he refused guns and reinforcements claiming he needed no aid against these Indians. Last, but not least, is his division of manpower into several smaller battalions, thus weakening his offensive line.

The Battle of Little Bighorn was later dubbed "Custer's Last Stand." It lasted just two days, June 25–26. It was the biggest victory for the Indians of the entire Plains Indian War, which was long and bloody. Despite this win at Little Big Horn, the Indians eventually lost their land. It was another five years, but they all ended up on designated reservations. Crazy Horse was killed when he left the reservation without permission from the US government. Sitting Bull was killed in 1890 by a policeman who was trying to arrest him because the US government was fearful of another uprising.

Sitting Bull, Lakota Indian Chief

About the Haunted Battlefield

According to legend, Indians scalped all the soldiers they killed at the Battle of Little Big Horn, according to their beliefs and customs. If this gruesome beheading did indeed happen, it could explain why this area is reportedly haunted. Or it may be because many men were buried in a mass grave and did not receive a proper burial. Or it may be the result of so many corpses being exhumed and reburied elsewhere. Disturbing the dead can cause paranormal activity.

Visitors have heard the anguished screams of soldiers, as well as chanting. Some believe that Custer haunts this site. Others believe it is haunted by the spirits of Indian warriors who ride their phantom horses through the battlefield on occasion. Many have claimed to have heard muffled voices and felt cold spots while visiting Last Stand Hill. Cold spots are when there is an extreme drop in temperature for no apparent reason. It is popularly believed to be a sign of supernatural activity. A few folks swear they have seen fighting along Battle Ridge.

A psychic who visited in the late 1980s claimed she felt the presence of soldiers' spirits when she was near the 7th Cavalry Monument. She also said she saw a soldier ride past the visitor's center and disappear at Cemetery Ridge. She also saw the spirits of more than two dozen Indians wearing full warrior dress including magnificent feathered headbands and brightly painted faces.

A park ranger named Mardell Plainfeather once saw a couple of Indian warriors atop their mounts. They were dressed for battle and had bows and shields.

A place where paranormal activity is often reported is the Stone House. This structure, which is located near the cemetery entrance, dates back to 1894 when it was built as a residence for the park's superintendent. The lower level was once used as a holding area for bodies awaiting burial. Today, it is the White Swan Memorial Library, which also has conference rooms and an office.

Staff has seen lights on inside the house when it was unoccupied and they knew that no one had left any lights on. A staff member, Neil Mangum, lived in the Stone House while searching for a permanent residence. The family dog was unusually skittish and acted strangely during the few weeks the Mangum family was there. On one occasion, Mangum was unable to get inside the house. Unsure what to do, he left, and then returned a short while later. The front door opened immediately.

But these events pale in comparison to the apparition that has been seen coming down the stairs. It is a woman in a long robe or dress. Phantom footsteps are another disturbing thing that happens from time to time. On one occasion, a ranger awoke sensing a presence. He glanced over and saw that his wife was asleep beside him. Unable to shake the eerie feeling he had, he began looking around and was frightened to find a shadowy figure perched at the foot of his bed. It appeared to be the torso of a soldier. He rubbed his eyes in disbelief. When he opened his eyes, the spooky specter had vanished!

Other staff members who have stayed in the house say they have heard banging and knocking that always stops as mysteriously as it begins. One couple often found their belongings had been moved. They believed it was a mischievous spirit so they were never worried. They grew accustomed to the activity, but just to be on the safe side, they put a crucifix in each room.

Just before the Stone House was converted to a library, four staff members spent the night in the old house. Loud footsteps were heard by the lady sleeping downstairs. She thought it was the men upstairs getting up to go to the bathroom or get a drink of water. But when the sounds continued for an unreasonably long period of time, she began to wonder what was going on. When the kitchen door slammed shut so violently that it shook the house, she quickly exited. She spent the rest of the night in her car. She shared what had happened with the men who had slept upstairs, but none of them had heard anything and all swore they slept soundly, meaning they did not get up during the night.

But that's not the only haunted building here. The staff at the visitor center have had scary encounters in the museum basement, including seeing shadowy figures who disappear through the door leading into the inventory room. Their descriptions are always the same. It is a man in a uniform with an old-time handlebar mustache and plaintive eyes. Rangers have confessed to being tapped on the shoulder and feeling something tugging at their leg by an unseen presence.

Ghostly activity has also been reported at Reno's Crossing, which is a few miles from Custer's Last Stand. It is where Marco Reno and his men retreated across the Little Bighorn River. In fact, folks who have seen and heard the strange things that happen here claim that Reno's Crossing is the most haunted spot in the whole park.

A chromolithograph dated 1899, artist unknown

Gold Rush

FYI: The Indian Wars took place from approximately the mid-1800s to 1890 because the government tried to force the Indians off their native land and onto designated reservations. According to the U.S. Census Bureau, there were as many as 40 skirmishes between the U.S. military and the American Indians from the earliest colonial settlements until 1890. The Civil War years, the railroad, Manifest Destiny, and the Gold Rush brought increased conflict between the Indians and the US government. This culminated in a final skirmish between the military and the Indians at the Battle of Wounded Knee, South Dakota, on December 29, 1890.

Chalmette National Battlefield & National Cemetery

Chalmette National Battlefield

& National Cemetery

Location: Chalmette, Louisiana

Established: Chalmette Monument and Grounds was established by the US War Department on March 4, 1907 and transferred to the National Park Service on August 10, 1933. Seven years later it was renamed the Chalmette National Historical Park. The park became part of the Jean Lafitte National Historic Park and Preserve on November 10, 1978.

The following is a list of six sites that comprise Jean Lafitte National Historic Park, which are located throughout southern Louisiana:

- Acadian Cultural Center (501 Fisher Road, Lafayette)
- Barataria Preserve (6588 Barataria Boulevard, Marrero)
- **Chalmette Battlefield and National Cemetery** (8606 West St. Bernard Highway, Chalmette)
- French Quarter Visitor Center (419 Decatur Street, New Orleans)
- Prairie Acadian Cultural Center (250 West Park Avenue, Eunice)
- Wetlands Acadian Cultural Center (314 St. Mary Street, Thibodaux)

Visitor Information

This battlefield and cemetery are open every day from 8:00 a.m. to 5:00 p.m. except on Thanksgiving, Christmas Day, and New Year's Day. There are no admission fees. The park headquarters is in the same building as the French Quarter Visitor's Center in New Orleans. Seasonal events include re-enactments and ranger programs.

Chalmette Battlefield can be reached from New Orleans French Quarter on the paddle wheeler *Creole Queen*. This is not only a fun way to get to the battlefield but also a great sightseeing cruise. Pets are not allowed in Chalmette National Cemetery, but leashed pets can go into Chalmette Battlefield. Pets may not be left unattended in vehicles for any period of time.

The Beauregard House is on the battlefield grounds. It is a museum and visitor center. Interestingly, this plantation was never used as a plantation. It was built in 1830 for Rene Beauregard, who was the son of Civil War General P.G.T. Beauregard (Confederacy).

Another place of interest for visitors is the Confederate Civil War Museum, which is located in downtown New Orleans. 929 Camp Street.

8606 West St. Bernard Highway

Chalmette, LA 70043 (six miles SE of New Orleans)

www.nps.gov/jela

The Battle of New Orleans by Henry Bryan Hall

About the Haunted Battlefield

This battlefield was the site of the Battle of New Orleans. Soldiers from the Civil War, Spanish-American War, Vietnam War, and World Wars I & II are buried in the adjacent cemetery, including four Americans who fought in the War of 1812, but only one participated in the Battle of New Orleans.

The Battle of New Orleans was actually the final conflict of the War of 1812. The War of 1812 was initiated by the British, who tried to reclaim the American colonies, which they lost after losing the American Revolutionary War. The conflict lasted for roughly thirty months before ending with the signing of the Treaty of Ghent on December 24, 1814, which was ratified by Congress on February 17, 1815. Even though the war was over, there were some issues left unresolved. However, the US considered it another victory in our battle for independence.

During this second showdown with Britain, General Andrew Jackson commanded a brave group of men against the British, who were led by General Pakenham. The British leader died on January 8, 1815 at the Battle of New Orleans.

The first campaign of this battle was the Battle of Lake Champlain in September 1814. The second campaign included the British burning the White House and the Capitol. The third began in late December and continued until January 8, 1815.

British General Pakenham led 10,000 troops from Lake Borgne to New Orleans. On December 23, Jackson stopped the British cold in a surprising night attack. They were less than nine miles from New Orleans when attacked and defeated. His plan was to capture this key port, thereby controlling the Mississippi River. This would cripple the US war efforts.

What makes this battle so remarkable is that most of the men who fought were not soldiers, although some were accustomed to battle. The "army" was comprised of 5,000 militia and volunteers, such as Pirate Captain Jean Lafitte and his band of Buccaneers.

Jean Lafitte

The Battle of New Orleans was considered the greatest land win of the War of 1812. It was also the last war in which the United States battled England. Today, they are considered one of our greatest allies. Furthermore, it made General Jackson a hero and led to his presidency (1829–1837).

It also resulted in an influx of residents to Louisiana and reunited our great nation. It is also important to point out that two volunteer battalions of free men of color fought in the Battle of New Orleans. They were the first African-American soldiers to receive the same amount of pay, pensions, equipment, and land grants as white soldiers received.

A lot of paranormal activity has been reported here. There has been so much strange goings on that several ghost groups have conducted investigations, such as Southern Area Paranormal Society. They have picked up lots of unexplainable EVPs. Additionally, the following has been reported by numerous credible witnesses:

*cannon fire is heard

*soldiers shouting battle commands

*whispers (in cemetery)

*sightings of British soldiers (in cemetery)

*cold spots

*being grabbed or pulled by an invisible hand

*inside the Beauregard House the sound of phantom footsteps on the stairs is sometimes heard and shadows have been seen along the walls

*weird photo anomalies, such as orbs, strange shadows, and mists

Chalmette National Cemetery extends more than 17 acres and is the final resting place for more than 15,000 veterans who fought in various wars, ranging from the Civil War to the Vietnam War. There are four graves for War of 1812 soldiers, but only one of those men died at the Battle of New Orleans.

Terrance Zepke

Valley Forge National Historic Park

Valley Forge National Historic Park

Washington and Layette at Valley Forge

"Naked and starving as they are we cannot enough admire the incomparable patience and fidelity of the soldiery." —General George Washington February 16, 1778, Valley Forge

Location: Valley Forge, Pennsylvania

Established: It became a state park in 1893 and on July 4, 1976 Valley Forge National Historic Park was established.

Visitor Information

The nearly 5.5-mile Valley Forge National Historic Park includes historical structures and replicas, as well as a visitor's center (including a Children's Exploration Station), carillon, and Washington Memorial Chapel. The park, which is open daily year-round, has walking and biking trails. There is no admission fee for the park. The visitor's center is open daily from 9:00 a.m. to 5:00 p.m. or 6:00 p.m. during the summer months. It is closed on Thanksgiving, Christmas Day, and New Year's Day. The center offers an orientation film and exhibits. Optional activities include a trolley tour, public or private tours, and seasonal events including re-enactments, bird watching, and photography programs. Ghost investigations and other special activities are allowed, but typically require a Special Use Permit.

1400 North Outer Line Drive
King of Prussia, PA 19406
www.nps.gov/vafo

Valley Forge National Historic Park is twenty miles northwest of Philadelphia, which is the location of Independence National Historic Park (home of the Liberty Bell). This park is free and open to the public. www.nps.gov/inde/index.htm

For more visitor information, go to www.valleyforge.org

About the Haunted Battlefield

Although no battle was fought here, Valley Forge has great historical significance. It was one of the most defining non-battle moments in our history. It was a turning point in the Revolutionary War. This is where the Continental Army, led by George Washington, spent a long, hard winter during the Revolutionary War, from December 19, 1777 to June 18, 1778.

More than 2,500 men died from starvation, disease, and freezing temperatures. Many of the men suffered from the flu, typhoid, and dysentery. Dysentery is an intestinal inflammation caused by an infection (induced by bacteria, virus, parasitic worms, or protozoa). It causes mild to severe diarrhea, fever, and abdominal pain. Most of the men were not adequately clothed for the harsh winter they faced. Some reports indicate that only one-third of the men had shoes upon arrival.

The back story is that Washington had been defeated in two key battles and lost the key city of Philadelphia. Still, Washington knew his men were up to the task of winning this war. They just needed more training. And winter afforded them that time. Both sides retreated to their respective camps. For several reasons, Washington was forced to choose Valley Forge as his winter encampment. Ironically, the opposing forces were just twenty miles from each other.

The Continental Army did the best they could with what they had, which wasn't much. Washington put Nathanael Greene in charge of the supplies. They built log cabins, trenches, forts and a bridge over Schuylkill River. They made clothing and gear using what meager supplies they had or could find. Greene had some success in finding food and clothing—both equally important. Many of the men were practically wearing rags by now (some didn't even have shoes) and all were suffering starvation. Their main nourishment was a broth and bread. Still, their spirits were high. They trained for long hours every day.

This training was key to future success because these men were not soldiers. They were tough and determined but had received no formal training. They had been enticed into battle with land grants and monetary bonuses. Most were also motivated by their desire for independence. Prussian Drill Master, Baron Friedrich von Steuben, was sent to lead the training efforts. He is responsible for turning these men into soldiers.

Replicas of the original cabins

What many people aren't aware of is the fact that there were women and children at Valley Forge. The women came to support their husbands, fathers, and brothers. They were known as Camp Followers and in addition to being so important for morale, they accomplished many important tasks, such as laundry, cooking, sewing, and nursing.

After repeated pleas from Washington and an official visit from a Congressional envoy, Congress finally sent supplies at the end of February.

On February 6, 1778, the US entered into an alliance with France. They agreed to send troops and money for the cause. This news sent the British packing. They fled Philadelphia in June in advance of the arriving French troops.

As a result of their winter training at Valley Forge, Washington and his men won the Battle of Monmouth on June 28. In fact, many believe the American Army was born at Valley Forge.

 George Washington's wife, Martha, arrived at Valley Forge on February 10, 1778. She worked hard to keep up morale by visiting the men in their huts and the makeshift camp hospital. She also organized the women (reportedly about 500) to create a sewing circle. They did an amazing job patching socks, pants, and shirts. Despite their efforts, they received half the food rations the men got and half the pay for their services.

With so much suffering and death here, it is no surprise that paranormal activity has been reported in this 3,600-acre park. In addition to all the men who died of disease and starvation, there was a spy who was hanged here. A man has been seen hanging from a tree on occasion. Those who see this horrific sight get so distraught that they run to find aid. By the time they find a ranger and return, the hanging victim has disappeared. This eerie sight is believed to be the spirit of the hanged spy. Also, witnesses have claimed to have seen campfires burning, singing, moaning, and soldiers (sentries) walking around. While seen by many folks over the years, these events have only been witnessed during the winter. Paranormal activity has been recorded by ghost groups, such as Tri-County Paranormal.

Isaac Potts House (Washington's Headquarters)

Fredericksburg and Spotsylvania National Military Park

Fredericksburg and Spotsylvania National Military Park

The Battle of Fredericksburg **by Kurz and Allison**

Location: Fredericksburg, Virginia

Established: This military park was established by the US War Department on February 14, 1927. It became part of the NPS on August 10, 1933.

Chancellorsville Battlefield

Visitor Information

This military park is comprised of four major Civil War battlefields in which the Battle of Fredericksburg, Battle of Chancellorsville, Battle of the Wilderness, and Battle of Spotsylvania Court House took place over the span of eighteen months and resulted in roughly 100,000 casualties. It includes five significant historic buildings: Chatham Manor, Salem Church, Ellwood, and the house where Stonewall Jackson died, as well as the ruins of the Chancellor mansion. There are two visitor centers at Fredericksburg and Chancellorsville. Exhibit shelters can be found at Wilderness and Spotsylvania Court House.

This park is the second largest military park in the world, encompassing more than 8,000 acres, so be sure to allow enough time to explore it. The 12-acre Fredericksburg National Cemetery adjoins the park. Both visitor centers are open year-round during the day except on Thanksgiving, Christmas Day, and New Year's Day. There are some good walking trails within this park including a 7-mile trail at Spotsylvania and a 2-mile trail at Wilderness.

Innis House and Sunken Road

Orientation films are offered at Fredericksburg and Chancellorsville. Additionally, a 30-minute guided "Sunken Road Walking Tour" is offered at Fredericksburg and a half-hour "Jackson Wounded Walking Tour" is offered at Chancellorsville. There is no fee to enter the park or for parking but there is a small fee charged for these films. Or you may opt to take a self-guided tour of the park. Visitors can rent or buy an audio at the Fredericksburg or Spotsylvania visitor centers to listen to while on their driving tour. Special events and ranger programs are offered seasonally. Richmond National Battlefield Park and Manassas National Battlefield Park are less than 60 miles away.

www.nps.gov/frsp

Battle of the Wilderness commemorative postage stamp

Fredericksburg Battlefield Visitor Center: 1013 Lafayette Boulevard, Fredericksburg, VA 22401

Chancellorsville Battlefield Visitor Center: 9001 Plank Road, Spotsylvania, VA 22553

Wilderness Battlefield Exhibit Shelter: 35347 Constitution Highway, Locust Grove, VA 22508

Spotsylvania Battlefield Exhibit Shelter: 9550 Grant Drive West, Spotsylvania, VA 22553

Battle of the Wilderness on Orange C.H. Plank Road, near Todd's Tavern, May 6th, 1864

About the Haunted Battlefields

The first of these four battles was the Battle of Fredericksburg (December 11–15, 1862). Next came the Battle of Chancellorsville (April 30–May 6, 1863). The Battle of Wilderness took place from May 5–7, 1863, and the last to occur was the Battle of Spotsylvania (May 8–21, 1863).

The **Battle of Fredericksburg** was a 5-day battle. It was one of the biggest and bloodiest battles of the war. More than 200,000 soldiers fought in the streets, at the river, and across acres of farmlands. The combatants were Confederate General Robert E. Lee's Army of Northern Virginia and Union Major General Ambrose Burnside's Army of the Potomac. Burnside's offensive against entrenched Confederates failed miserably. More than 11,000 lives were lost as a result of this campaign with most being Union soldiers. It is considered one of the most one-sided battles of the Civil War. President Lincoln stripped Burnside of his command within weeks of this battle.

The Battle of Chancellorsville occurred from April 30, 1863–May 6, 1863. It began with a plan concocted by both Stonewall Jackson and Robert E. Lee. This was considered to be one of the riskiest battle plans of the war. But they needed a bold plan to stop Major General Hooker from attacking Lee's vulnerable flank. Jackson led 30,000 men to attack Hooker's flank, which was determined to be its weakest. The surprise attack worked in that it was a total surprise to Hooker and his men. Unfortunately, it resulted in the death of one of the best leaders of the Confederacy, Stonewall Jackson. Despite the setback, Lee managed to defeat the Federal forces near Salem Church. Had he not done so when he had, they would have surely attacked his vulnerable flank, which would have resulted in many lost lives and the loss of an important battle. Lee's victory at Chancellorsville was one of the biggest and best outcomes of the whole war. It has been analyzed and praised by military experts throughout the years.

The Battle of Wilderness began on May 5, 1863. Once again, Lee's Army of Northern Virginia clashed with Grant's Army of the Potomac. The fighting took place in a densely wooded area of Spotsylvania County. After two days of fighting, Grant withdrew and continued his march to the south. Despite this retreat, this was not a victory for the Confederates but rather another stalemate of many in this long war.

The Battle of Spotsylvania occurred from May 8–21, 1864 in Spotsylvania County, Virginia. It began on May 7 when General Grant ordered the Army of the Potomac to go to Spotsylvania Court House, a small town near Richmond, Virginia. Grant was hoping to finally defeat Lee's Army of Northern Virginia. But first he had to get past General Stuart's troops. They had to hold Laurel Hill if they were to keep the Federal forces from reaching Lee. If they lost, they lost control of Spotsylvania and any hope of stopping the progression of Army of the Potomac. Heavy fighting continued for three days during which time the highest ranking officer of the Union was killed, Major General John Sedgwick.

The Confederacy had built a strong line of earthworks, including Mule Shoe Salient, which became known as Bloody Angle. By mid-May, General Grant attacked this area, which he felt was the weakest part of the Confederate line. He was right, but it was not an easy victory. A terrible storm, lasting nearly 24 hours, erupted and created some tough conditions. Thousands of lives were lost before this battle finally ended on May 21. And, even though, the Union troops outnumbered the Confederates 2:1, they lost close to the same number of soldiers. Approximately 18,000 Federal soldiers were killed, missing or wounded while the Confederacy suffered a loss of 13,000. This is yet another battle of the American Civil War that had an inconclusive ending, meaning that neither side gained any advantage from the skirmish.

Because so much fighting and bloodshed was done here, it is easy to see why it has so much paranormal activity. Witnesses have reported many incidents over the years. A band of soldiers has been seen walking around the cemetery.

The most haunted place in the park is Bloody Angle. Lots of folks have reported strange incidents here. In addition to lots of individual witnesses, a half dozen paranormal groups, such as Powhatan and Tri-Mar Paranormal Research, have also reported activity.

Here are the results of Tri-Mar's investigation:

1. **Spotsylvania Court House Battlefield:** Reported to be one of the most haunted battlefields in America. Daytime investigation of the 1864 battlefield including: "Bloody Angle," "McCoull House Site," "East Face of Salient," and "Landrum House Site." Elevated EMF readings were noted at Bloody Angle, Landrum House, and McCoull House. Fredericksburg Area Paranormal Investigations collected EVP evidence at the McCoull House Site.

2. **Chancellorsville Battlefield:** Daytime investigation of the 1863 battlefield including: "Hazel Grove," "Fairview," "Jackson's Flank Attack," "Chancellor House / Chancellorsville Inn Site," and "Chancellorsville First Day." Fredericksburg Area Paranormal Investigations collected EVP evidence at Fairview and at the ruins.

3. **Wilderness Battlefield:** Two-day daytime investigation of the 1864 battlefield including: "Gordon's Flank Attack," "Saunders Field," "Higgerson Farm," "Chewning Farm," "Tapp Field," and "Brock Road / Orange Plank Road Intersection." Elevated EMF readings were noted at Chewning and Higgerson Farms and along the Brock Road trenches. Orb activity photographed at Tapp Field on both days. Ellwood was partially investigated in September, including the burial site of Stonewall Jackson's amputated arm. No Results.

4. **Fredericksburg Battlefield:** Daytime investigation of the 1862 battlefield including: "Marye's Heights," "Sunken Road," and "Prospect Hill." Moderate and steady EMF readings on Sunken Road in front of Brompton.

5. **Chatham Manor:** An extension of the Fredericksburg Battlefield. Not investigated.

6. **Slaughter Pen Farm**: A privately owned extension of the Fredericksburg Battlefield. No results.

7. **Old Salem Church:** Daytime investigation of this extension of the Chancellorsville Battlefield. No results.

8. **Stonewall Jackson Shrine:** Death site of the general after the Battle of Chancellorsville. Minor K-II reading near the parking area.

Appomattox Court House National Historical Park

Appomattox Court House National Historical Park

Reconstructed Appomattox Courthouse

Location: Appomattox, Virginia

Established: The 1,325-acre park was established on August 3, 1935 and later became a national historical park in 1954.

Visitor Information

This military park and visitor's center are open daily year-round except for national holidays. There is a small fee to enter the park, but the fee is waived if you have a valid National Park Pass. It is recommended that visitors allow two hours to adequately explore the historic village, which became a National Historic Landmark in 1940.

There is a 100-yard uphill walk from the parking lot to the village. There are no paved areas in the village, only gravel and grassy areas. Furthermore, the villages are not handicap-accessible so be advised that wheelchairs will not fit through most of the doorways or down narrow hallways and there are no ramps, only steps.

The visitor's center offers a museum with lots of exhibits on the second floor. There isn't an elevator, but there is a photo album of these exhibits on the main level. Also, there are two short films. It is recommended that you start at the visitor's center where you can watch these orientation films and pick up a free park map. There is a bookstore and gift shop in the Tavern Kitchen. Seasonal events are offered, such as living history talks and ranger programs including year-round junior ranger programs.

Podcast and cell phone tours are available. Information for these options can be found on www.np.gov/apco. There is an Appomattox Battle App, which will guide you to all the historic spots on the battlefield, the town, and the site where Lee surrendered to Grant.

iOS: www.civilwar.org/appomattoxapp

Android: www.civilwar.org/appomattoxandroid

While you're in the area, you may want to visit **The Museum of the Confederacy-Appomattox**. Visitors can see artifacts, photographs, and documents relating to the Civil War. www.moc.org

The museum houses a replica of the parlor and the scene of the surrender. Grant sat at the wooden table and Lee sat at the marble-topped table.

111 National Park Dr.

Appomattox Court House, Virginia 24522 (95 miles west of Richmond)

www.nps.gov/apco or for general tourism info: www.historicappomattox.com

 **Ulysses S. Grant**

Commanding General of the US Army and 18th President of the US.

About the Haunted Battlefield

Confederate General Robert E. Lee arrived at Appomattox on April 8. He was trying to reach Appomattox Station to meet a food supply train but was thwarted at every turn. In a last ditch effort, he tried to retreat via the Appomattox River but realized he was surrounded by Union troops. There wasn't much of a Battle of Appomattox. There was a brief skirmish that morning, but Lee soon knew that he was outmanned and to pursue any military action would have resulted in many casualties with no possibility of victory. He had no choice but to surrender the following day.

While it is true that Lee surrendered on April 9, 1865, there was no treaty signed that day. This was strictly a military surrender but the Confederate government never officially surrendered. If they had, the US government would have been acknowledging the existence of another government. This was impossible since it would have accorded the Confederate government some legal status and protection.

Once Lee realized that surrender was inevitable, he sent a letter to General Grant. In his letter, he requested a meeting to discuss the terms of surrender. Grant agreed to the meeting and even left the details to Lee. After some consideration, a location was finalized.

Lee surrendered to Grant on April 9, 1865 in a private residence in Appomattox Court House, Virginia. It was a cordial meeting between two great generals. They rehashed their initial introduction, which was during the Mexican War. After about a half hour, they got down to business. The entire meeting lasted roughly an hour and a half.

The owner of the property, William McLean, was recorded that day as saying, "The war started in my front yard and ended in my front parlor."

McLean had left Manassas, Virginia when General Beauregard set up headquarters on his property, which also served as the perimeter of the battlefield.

McLean House (April 1865)

Grant graciously agreed to pardon all Confederate officers and enlisted men, but all arms had to be relinquished. (They were officially relinquished on April 12.) Many men in the Army of Northern Virginia were riding their own mules or horses. Grant agreed to let those men keep their mounts and swords. Grant even agreed to feed the hungry Confederates, who had been without rations for a few days.

Men from both sides cheered when the announcement was made as it had been a long, hard four years. Union troops saluted their former enemies at the conclusion of the surrender ceremony.

General Lee never offered his sword to General Grant, and Grant never demanded it. Both men showed great character during this final resolution to the Civil War. In fact, this event has become known as "The

Gentlemen's Agreement."

Despite the pardons given on this day, many demanded that Lee and other Confederate leaders be arrested and tried for treason. Grant was adamant that Lee could not be tried as he had been officially pardoned.

Even though Lee surrendered, the war was still not over. It was another two weeks before General Johnston surrendered his army to General Sherman on April 26. The final battle of the Civil War took place in Texas on May 11–12. The last large Confederate military force was surrendered on June 2 by General Edmund Kirby Smith in Galveston, Texas.

Confederate President Jefferson Davis was captured in Georgia on May 10. He was imprisoned for two years on charges of treason. However, he never went to trial. The government finally realized that trying Davis on these grounds might lend support to the constitutionality of secession.

 **Robert E. Lee**

Superintendent of US Military Academy, General of the Army of Northern Virginia, and President of Washington and Lee University; served in Mexican-American War, Harpers Ferry, and Civil War

Here is a copy of orders General Robert E. Lee wrote to his men on April 10, 1865:

After four years of arduous service marked by unsurpassed courage and fortitude, the Army of Northern Virginia has been compelled to yield to overwhelming numbers and resources. I need not tell the survivors of so many hard-fought battles, who have remained steadfast to the last, that I have consented to the result from no distrust of them. But feeling that valor and devotion could accomplish nothing that could compensate for the loss that must have attended the continuance of the contest, I have determined to avoid the useless sacrifice of those whose past services have endeared them to their countrymen. By the terms of the agreement, officers and men can return to their homes and remain until exchanged. You will take with you the satisfaction that proceeds from the consciousness of duty faithfully performed, and I earnestly pray that a merciful God will extend to you his blessing and protection. With an unceasing admiration of your constancy and devotion to your Country, and a grateful remembrance of your kind and generous consideration for myself, I bid you an affectionate farewell.

— R. E. Lee, General, *General Order No. 9*

"The Surrender" by Keith Rocco shows the known officers that were present for at least a portion of the meeting in the McLean Parlor, April 9, 1865.

The officers in this painting are from left to right:

Lt. Col. Charles Marshall
Lt. Col. Ely S. Parker
Gen. Robert E. Lee
Lt. Col. Orville E. Babcock
Lt. Gen. Ulysses S. Grant
Maj. Gen. Edward O. C. Ord
Lt. Col. Horace Porter
Capt. Robert T. Lincoln
Lt. Col. Theodore S. Bowers
Maj. Gen. Phillip H. Sheridan
Brig. Gen. John Rawlins
Brig. Gen. Rufus Ingalls
Lt. Col. Adam Badeau

Brig. Gen. George H. Sharpe
Brig. Gen. Michael Morgan
Brig. Gen. Seth Williams

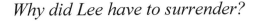

Why did Lee have to surrender?

One big reason is that he lost more than half his men
during the Siege of Petersburg when they were captured,
killed, or deserted. The final straw was his being unable to
escape from Grant on April 8. If he had been able to reach
the supply train or General Johnston (who had an army of
90,000), there might have been a different outcome to this
war. Some of his men wanted to fight until the bitter end,
but Lee felt there had been enough loss of lives during this
four-year war.

Even though there was not much fighting done here, it
was one of the most significant events in this war.

The most haunted place in Appomattox is the
Crawford Farm, which is near Falling River. Legend
has it that Elijah Crawford was a soldier in the Civil

War and also a plantation owner. But unlike other plantations, he didn't use slave labor. He freed his slaves before the Civil War. The freed slaves became paid workers, so he had no problems finding help after the war as he had lots of loyal workers. His plantation thrived and he became a very wealthy man. He was blessed to also be deeply in love with his wife. The couple had a child, Amos, and they were very happy. His wife, Alice, eventually became pregnant with their second child, Abigail. Sadly, she died in childbirth. Elijah Crawford was devastated by his wife's death. To this day, crying and anguished moaning can be heard here.

But that's not all. When Elijah's daughter, Abigail, died less than six years later from fever, Elijah lost it. He begged a former slave, a Haitian woman who was skilled in the art of black magic, to help him contact and hopefully resurrect his dead wife and daughter. Obsessed with this plan, Crawford shut down the farm to devote his full attention to this plan.

Interestingly, several people died mysterious deaths or disappeared on or around Crawford farm. Nothing could be tied to Elijah, however, until his nurse was found dead. It was discovered that she died of poisoning and appeared to have been subjected to some kind of voodoo ritual as she was found strapped to a table with her eyes sewn shut and strange herbs on her tongue. These same herbs and many more were found in jars under Crawford's bed.

But the authorities could not locate Crawford. It was two weeks before he was found hanged from a neighbor's tree. It remains a mystery how, despite being in ill health, he managed to elude authorities and get more than two miles away and hang himself from a tall tree without any evident aid.

The coroner found a journal written by Elijah Crawford that disturbed him so deeply that he removed vital organs from the dead man's body, presumably to keep him from being able to return from the afterlife. The coroner feared the man had discovered a portal to the dark side.

His remains were taken to the Crawford farm, but he was not given a proper burial. However, the Daughters of the Confederacy eventually buried his remains in the family cemetery.

In addition to inexplicable crying and moaning, spirits have been seen roaming around the property. One is believed to be Abigail because she is seen carrying a doll and Abigail used to love to play with dolls. Another scary looking specter is believed to be Amos Crawford, whose arm was cut off by angry loggers in retribution for an injury caused by Amos. An even spookier spirit is believed to be that of Jonesy Letts, a farmer who died of fever but not before the blisters disfigured his face.

Other spirits that may haunt this property may be some of the folks who turned up dead (including Nurse Sarah Caldwell) or missing over the years, a ghost dog, a moonshiner, a witch, and a woman who died when she fell down the hill.

Even if this legend has been exaggerated over time, the strange sights and sounds that have been witnessed by many cannot be disputed.

FYI: The **American Civil War** has also been referred to as:

War Between the States, War of the Rebellion, Great Rebellion, War of Northern Aggression, War for Southern Independence, Freedom War, and **War of Secession.**

Terrance Zepke

Richmond National Battlefield Park

Richmond National Battlefield Park

Location: Mechanicsville, Virginia

Established: March 2, 1936

Visitor Information

This military park preserves more than 2,200 acres of Civil War sites that include 30 sites around Richmond, Virginia including Hanover, Henrico, and Chesterfield Counties. Three noteworthy places in this park are:

1. **Cold Harbor Battlefield & Visitor Center**
   Open 9:00 a.m. to 4:30 p.m. daily except Thanksgiving, Christmas Day, and New Year's Day. Features related exhibits and artifacts. The visitor's center includes an electric map program for Cold Harbor and Gaines's Mill, exhibits, and a small bookstore. A one-mile drive parallels and crosses significant stretches of both the Confederate and Union entrenchments, all of which are original to 1864. A series of walking trails, ranging from one mile to nearly three miles, takes visitors through the site in greater detail. Numerous signs enhance the visit. 5515 Anderson-Wright Drive, five miles southeast of Mechanicsville on route 156.

2. **Civil War Visitor's Center at Tredegar Iron Works**
   Open 9:00 am to 5:00 p.m. daily except for the same holidays as above. 470 Tredegar Street, Richmond. The visitor's center has

a bookstore/gift shop and three floors of exhibits and a film. There is a self-guided driving tour. A map and/or a CD audio tour may be used. The NPS recommends four hours to do this tour. There are podcasts for visitors, as well. The main visitor's center occupies one of the surviving buildings that made up the Tredegar Iron Works—the Confederacy's leader in the production of artillery, ammunition and war-related materials. Inside are three floors of exhibits including interactive map programs, displays on the Richmond military and home front along with the park's orientation film to Richmond's battlefields. The grounds contain machinery and related exhibits that address more than one hundred years of iron making at Tredegar. Within walking distance are sections of the rebuilt James River and Kanawha Canal, Brown's Island where women and children produced ammunition, and Belle Isle, site of a prisoner-of-war camp for thousands of Union troops.

3. **Chimborazo Medical Museum**
   Open 9:00 a.m. to 4:30 p.m. daily except the same holidays as above. 3215 East Broad Street, Richmond, Virginia, 23223. The museum offers exhibits about the

medical equipment and tenure of Chimborazo Hospital. Chimborazo became one of the Civil War's largest military hospitals. When completed, it contained more than one hundred wards, a bakery, and even a brewery. Although the hospital no longer exists, a museum on the same grounds contains original medical instruments and personal artifacts. Other displays include a scale model of the hospital and a short film on medical and surgical practices and the caregivers that comforted the sick and wounded.

Pets are permitted in this park but not inside any buildings and they must be leashed. They cannot be left unattended at any time. Horseback riding and picnicking are permitted as per park rules. Camping and campfires are not allowed. Most of the park is handicap-accessible. There are no admission fees, but there is a small parking fee at the Civil War Visitor's Center at Tredegar Iron Works.

For more on this battlefield and all sites of interest, visit www.nps.gov/rich.

Battle of Cold Harbor by Kurz and Allison, 1888

About the Haunted Battlefield

Richmond National Battlefield Park commemorates more than thirty American Civil War battles that occurred around Richmond, Virginia. These skirmishes include Beaver Dam Creek, Cold Harbor, Drewery's Bluff, Gaines's Mill, Glendale, Malvern Hill, and New Market Heights.

The Battle of Cold Harbor was fought between May 31 and June 12, 1864. It is significant for several reasons. Naval military history was made at the battle of Drewery's Bluff. General Grant personally commanded Union troops during this battle. But despite his leadership, the battle was won by the Confederacy.

This was an important win since the prize was Richmond. General Lee fought his first battle at Beaver

Creek. However, both sides suffered heavy losses. It is estimated that more than 16,000 lives were lost (or badly wounded) during this two-week battle. Many civilian lives were lost due to disease and famine. Farms became battlefields, homes became hospitals, and cemeteries became an all too common part of the landscape.

Although there were many battles during the course of the Civil War, the Battle of Cold Harbor played a major role in this war. Just a few weeks before the Battle of Cold Harbor, President Lincoln visited Richmond. That was just days before his assassination.

The spirits of many soldiers are believed to still linger here. Visitors to the Richmond National Battlefield Park have reported seeing them in their uniforms. Sometimes it is a solitary soldier while other times a band of soldiers have been seen. The sound of horses' hooves, rifles and cannons firing, and ghostly whispers have also been reported. Even a mysterious fog has been reported on occasion.

Antietam National Battlefield

Antietam National Battlefield

Location: Sharpsburg, Maryland

Established: August 30, 1890

Visitor Information

Antietam National Battlefield is open every day during daylight hours except on Thanksgiving, Christmas, and New Year's Day. The battlefield is 17 miles from Harpers Ferry Historic Park, 60 miles from Gettysburg Battlefield, and 65 miles from Manassas Battlefield. The first thing you should do is to go to the visitor's center and watch a short introductory film.

The park service offers interpretive programs, seasonal events, and guided tours (www.antietamguides.com). There are a museum and cemetery in addition to the battlefield. The museum is inside the Pry House, which was Union General McClellan's headquarters during this battle. The Antietam National Cemetery extends more than eleven acres.

The best way to explore the park is to take a self-guided driving tour that includes eleven stops. Or you can do the 8.5-mile route on a bike or on foot. You can buy an audio in the gift shop that explains each stop on this route.

Camping is allowed by permit in a designated area, but picnicking is prohibited in the cemetery, inside the Dunker Church, in the Observation Tower, on the Burnside Bridge, or on any monument. Most recreational activities are not allowed except in the designated camping area. Firearms are not allowed anywhere in the park and neither is hunting. Pets must be leashed and attended at all times. Bicycling, fishing, and horseback riding are permitted with certain restrictions. www.nps.gov/anti

5831 Dunker Church Road

Sharpsburg, MD 21782

www.nps.gov/anti

Burnside's Bridge during *Battle of Antietam* by Kurz & Allison

About the Haunted Battlefield

This one-day battle resulted in the loss of roughly 23,000 men (killed, wounded, or missing). On September 17, 1862 the Battle of Antietam, which is also known as the Battle of Sharpsburg, was the first battle of the Civil War to occur on Union land. This was the Confederate Army's first invasion on northern soil. It was fought between the town of Sharpsburg, Maryland and Antietam Creek. The Battle of Antietam is also known as the bloodiest battle of the war because of the high loss of lives in such a short amount of time. To put this into perspective, this is only slightly less than the same number who died on D-Day during the Normandy Invasion in 1944.

It is hard to imagine this outcome given that a copy of General Lee's battle plans was discovered by two Union soldiers. They found Special Order 191 wrapped around three cigars! Lee's entire battle strategy was laid out and in the hands of his enemy. It revealed that he planned to divide his army, sending men to Harper's Ferry, West Virginia, and Hagerstown, Maryland. With this knowledge, victory would have been guaranteed if the Union had acted quickly upon this information.

But for some reason, General McClellan waited almost 18 hours before acting on this information. His actions were too little, too late. The Battle of Antietam began at sunrise and was over before sunset on September 17, 1862. There were no winners of this battle either. It is considered "tactically inconclusive." While Confederate troops did withdraw from the field first, the Union gained nothing from this skirmish. In fact, they lost 25 percent of their troops.

President Lincoln gave his Emancipation Proclamation shortly after this battle despite his disappointment in the outcome. He and many others believed that if McClellan had acted more decisively, this battle could have been the end for the Confederacy rather than a draw. Not only did McClellan blow it by not using Special Order 191 to his full advantage, he also ceased fighting when he could have easily stopped the Confederacy for good by using the 20,000 men he had in reserve to finish off Lee's Army of Northern Virginia. After having lost so many men, defeating Lee's remaining army wouldn't have been much of a challenge. But once again McClellan erred on the side of caution.

The underlying purpose of the timing of Lincoln's Emancipation Proclamation was to stop the French and British governments from supporting the Confederacy. All the lives lost during the Battle of Antietam definitely deterred England and France from getting involved.

With all this bloodshed, it is easy to see why it is considered one of the most haunted battlefields in our great nation. It would be a shorter list to detail what is not haunted within this historic site.

One of the most haunted areas is Bloody Lane. The most common occurrences are the sounds of gunfire and the smell of gunpowder. Black smoke has been seen from time to time before it disappears into the ether. A group of school children on a field trip told a park ranger they heard singing "Fa-la-la-la-la" while wandering around the field. The park guide thinks they heard *"Faugh a Ballagh!"* which is a Gaelic battle cry for the Irish Brigade. The brigade lost half their men during the Battle of Antietam. Confederate officers have been seen from time to time. They look so realistic that witnesses thought they were Civil War re-enactors right up until they vanished into thin air!

Inexplicable blue lights (also described as blue balls of light) are seen on occasion at Burnside Bridge, which is where many Union soldiers died and were buried. The final skirmish happened at this 125-foot long bridge over Antietam Creek. Losses totaled nearly 3,500 for the Union and Confederacy. When witnesses move closer to get a better look, the flickering bluish lights vanish. The sound of a phantom drum playing cadence is heard on occasion around the bridge.

Burnside's Bridge

The Pry House is believed to be haunted by General Richardson's wife, Frances. A woman in period clothing has been seen coming down the stairs before disappearing and has also been seen in the upstairs window, which was the room where her husband died. But some think it is also haunted by Richardson, who died inside the house as a result of battle wounds.

Ghost sightings and unexplainable activity have also taken place at St. Paul Episcopal Church, which was used as a Confederate hospital after this battle. Moaning, groaning, and wailing are sometimes heard here. Flickering lights have also been reported.

FYI: During the Battle of Antietam, a skirmish was fought at Sunken Road, which came to be known as "Bloody Lane" following this battle. Confederate soldiers were well positioned all along this clay road, lying in wait for Union soldiers. As the Union soldiers came over the rise, they were quickly gunned down by the enemy. Sunken Road soon looked more like a bloody lane than an old dirt road.

The Piper House was part of the battlefield and the headquarters of Confederate General Longstreet. Its barn was used as a hospital. Reports continue to this day of strange goings-on throughout this property. The former residence is now an inn. Guests have witnessed sightings and sounds, such as whispering voices and phantom footsteps. Paranormal activity increased after renovations were done, which included adding onto the house. This addition was done on top of graves, and some believe this has made the spirits restless.

Gettysburg National Military Park

Gettysburg National Military Park

Location: Gettysburg, Pennsylvania

Established: February 2, 1895

Visitor Information

The roughly 6,000-acre park is open year-round from sunrise to sunset. Visitors can explore independently or take a guided tour. Special events and ranger programs are offered seasonally. The best place to start is the visitor's center, which offers two special options: the Gettysburg Cyclorama and a 20-minute film narrated by actor Morgan Freeman. There is also a gift shop and Refreshment Saloon.

Additionally, the museum features one of the largest collections of Civil War relics in the world, as well as 12 museum galleries. Visitors may also explore the 17-acre Soldiers National Cemetery and the David Wills House.

More than one million people visit this park annually, making it one of the most visited parks in America. There are 1,328 memorials, monuments, and markers throughout the park, which gives it the distinction of having the largest outdoor collection of sculptures in the world.

1195 Baltimore Pike

Gettysburg, PA 17325

www.nps.gov/gett

This battle has significance for three reasons:

*It was the largest battle fought in North America.

*It was the bloodiest battle of the Civil War with 51,000 killed, wounded, missing, or captured.

*It was considered "The High Water Mark of the Rebellion."

About the Haunted Battlefield

It all began after General Robert E. Lee won the Battle of Chancellorsville. This motivated him to pursue a second invasion of the North, which was known as the Gettysburg Campaign. Major General George Meade's army met up with Lee's army just north of Gettysburg on July 1, 1863. Reinforcements arrived for both sides and the fighting continued into July 2. Heavy fighting took place throughout the day all over the area, including McPherson's Ridge, Oak Hill, Oak Ridge, Seminary Ridge, Barlow's Knoll, and in the town of Gettysburg.

The second day of the Battle of Gettysburg was the longest and costliest of this 3-day battle. It took place at Devil's Den, Little Round Top, the Peach Orchard, the Wheatfield, Cemetery Ridge, Trostle's Farm, Culp's Hill, and Cemetery Hill. Roughly, 100,000 soldiers were engaged in combat on July 2 and more than 20 percent of those men were dead, wounded, captured, or missing by the end of the day. This was one of the top ten bloodiest battles of the whole war. Day three (July 3) was the last day of this historic battle. It culminated with the now famous Pickett's Charge. The Confederacy attempted to break the Union line at Cemetery Ridge.

Roughly 12,000 Confederate soldiers charged the Union line. They were unsuccessful and suffered heavy casualties. General Lee had no choice but to beat a hasty retreat back to Virginia. The loss of this important battle was a turning point in the War Between the States. It was the beginning of the end for the Confederacy.

FYI: There were 120 generals at the Battle of Gettysburg. Nine died during the battle or as a result of battle wounds.

Soldiers National Cemetery

Since this was the bloodiest battle of the entire war, it is certainly not surprising that this is one of the most haunted battlefields. In fact, the hauntings extend across the town since fighting transpired all over the place. Over the years, there have been many reports of paranormal activity, such as encounters with soldier spirits and inexplicable sounds of artillery fire and battle cries. The most haunted places within the park are at Little Round Top, Slaughter Pen, and Devil's Den. If you want to hear stories about these hauntings, you need to hire a guide as the park rangers won't talk about them. They have been instructed not to although several former rangers have been candid about the paranormal encounters they had while working at the park.

According to legend, Devil's Den was haunted long before the bloody battle that took place on the second day of the Battle of Gettysburg. If it wasn't haunted before, it certainly was after this skirmish. Confederate corpses were left to rot for days (possibly weeks). Some may never have been buried but simply tossed into the deep crevices within Devil's Den. A Texan soldier has been seen on many occasions.

Other places that are part of the park that are well known to be haunted include the George Weikert House, Hummelbaugh House, and Rose Farm.

The most haunted places outside of the battlefield are Gettysburg College, Cashtown Inn, Jennie Wade House, and the Farnsworth House Inn. Twenty-year-old Jennie Wade was the only civilian casualty of the Battle of Gettysburg. She was killed when a musket ball smashed through her door, killing her instantly. Residents, realizing they could suffer the same fate, soon left their homes.

Visitors can see all the bullet holes that riddle the walls of Farnsworth Inn. One of the rooms has been padlocked to prevent anyone from entering. It was here that a couple of Confederate sharpshooters were posted. It is believed that one or both must have suffered a severe injury or possibly was killed in this room. The spirit or spirits that appear are considered to be mean spirits. There are several other haunted areas within the Farnsworth House.

Gettysburg College's Pennsylvania Hall was used as a field hospital and look-out post. Over the years, there have been numerous reports by staff and students who swear they have seen soldiers in the building's cupola as if on sentry duty. Yet whenever anyone, such as faculty or security, goes to investigate, they do not find anyone in or around the cupola.

There is one story that is quite disturbing if it is to be believed. One night, two women who worked in the administrative office were working late. When they finally finished up, they took the elevator down to the main level, as usual. However, the elevator did not stop on the first floor but descended to the basement, which had served as the operating theater during the war. The doors opened and revealed a horrifying sight. It looked as if they had stepped back in time to when it had been an operating area. It was a very chaotic scene filled with nurses scurrying around and bodies and blood everywhere. Surgeons wearing bloody aprons could also be seen. One looked up and gestured for them to come and help! They screamed and frantically punched the elevator button, which ascended to the first floor. Both women continued to work for the school but refused to ride the elevator or work late after that night.

 About the Gettysburg Address…

This was a short speech given by President Abraham Lincoln (pictured here) on November 19, 1863 when the Soldiers National Cemetery was dedicated. This was just a few months after the Battle of Gettysburg. It is considered to be one of the greatest speeches in American history.

The Gettysburg Address

Four score and seven years ago our fathers brought forth on this continent, a new nation, conceived in Liberty, and dedicated to the proposition that all men are created equal.

Now we are engaged in a great civil war, testing whether that nation, or any nation so conceived and so dedicated, can long endure. We are met on a great battlefield of that war. We have come to dedicate a portion of that field, as a final resting place for those who here gave their lives that that nation might live. It is altogether fitting and proper that we should do this.

But, in a larger sense, we cannot dedicate—we cannot consecrate—we cannot hallow—this ground. The brave men, living and dead, who struggled here, have consecrated it, far above our poor power to add or detract. The world will little note, nor long remember what we say here, but it can never forget what they did here. It is for us the living, rather, to be dedicated here to the unfinished work which they who fought here have thus far so nobly advanced. It is rather for us to be here dedicated to the great task remaining before us—that from these honored dead we take increased devotion to that cause for which they gave the last full measure of devotion—that we here highly resolve that these dead shall not have died in vain—that this nation, under God, shall have a new birth of freedom—and that government of the people, by the people, for the people, shall not perish from the earth.

"Hancock at Gettysburg" by Thure de Thulstrup (Pickett's Charge)

A Timeline of the Civil War...

(April 12, 1861 – April 9, 1865)

With the exception of the American Revolution, no war has been fought on American soil with greater consequences than the Civil War. Battles were fought from the Northeast to as far as New Mexico during the course of this four-year war. This was a long, hard-fought war with plenty of losses on both sides and a great toll was paid by an entire nation. Did you know that as many as 10,000 skirmishes were fought during this war? Civil War battles are divided into the Eastern, Western, and Trans-Mississippi Theaters.

Here is a list of major battles fought over the course of the Civil War:

1861: Eastern Theater

April 12-14 - Battle of Fort Sumter - South Carolina

June 3 - Battle of Philippi - Virginia

June 10 - Battle of Big Bethel - Virginia

July 21 - First Battle of Bull Run - Virginia

October 21 - Battle of Ball's Bluff - Virginia

November 8 - The Trent Affair - at Sea

1861 Western Theater

August 10 - Battle of Wilson's Creek - Missouri

November 7 - Battle of Belmont - Missouri

1862: Eastern Theater

March 8-9 - Battle of Hampton Roads - Virginia

March 23 - First Battle of Kernstown - Virginia

April 5 - Siege of Yorktown - Virginia

April 10-11 - Battle of Fort Pulaski - Georgia

May 8 - Battle of McDowell - Virginia

May 31 - Battle of Seven Pines - Virginia

June 8 - Battle of Cross Keys - Virginia

June 9 - Battle of Port Republic - Virginia

June 26 - Battle of Beaver Dam Creek (Mechanicsville) - Virginia

June 27 - Battle of Gaines's Mill - Virginia

June 29 - Battle of Savage's Station - Virginia

June 30 - Battle of Glendale (Frayser's Farm) - Virginia

July 1 - Battle of Malvern Hill - Virginia

September 15 - Battle of South Mountain - Maryland

September 17 - Battle of Antietam - Maryland

December 13 - Battle of Fredericksburg – Virginia

1862: Western Theater

January 19 - <u>Battle of Mill Springs</u> - Kentucky

February 6 - <u>Battle of Fort Henry</u> - Tennessee

February 11-16 - <u>Battle of Fort Donelson</u> - Tennessee

April 6-7 - <u>Battle of Shiloh</u> - Tennessee

April 12 - <u>Great Locomotive Chase</u> - Georgia

April 24/25 - <u>Capture of New Orleans</u> - Louisiana

June 6 - <u>Battle of Memphis</u> - Tennessee

September 19 - <u>Battle of Iuka</u> - Mississippi

October 3-4 - <u>Second Battle of Corinth</u> - Mississippi

October 8 - <u>Battle of Perryville</u> - Kentucky

December 26-29 - <u>Battle of Chickasaw Bayou</u> - Mississippi

December 31-January 2, 1863 - <u>Battle of Stones River</u> - Tennessee

1862: Trans-Mississippi Theater

February 21 - <u>Battle of Valverde</u> - New Mexico

March 7-8 - <u>Battle of Pea Ridge</u> - Arkansas

March 26-28 - <u>Battle of Glorieta Pass</u> - New Mexico

1863: Eastern Theater

May 1-6 - <u>Battle of Chancellorsville</u> - Virginia

June 9 - <u>Battle of Brandy Station</u> - Virginia

July 1-3 - <u>Battle of Gettysburg</u> - Pennsylvania

July 3 - <u>Battle of Gettysburg - Pickett's Charge</u> - Pennsylvania

July 11 & 18 - <u>Battles of Fort Wagner</u> - South Carolina

October 13-November 7 - <u>Bristoe Campaign</u> - Virginia

November 26-December 2 - <u>Mine Run Campaign</u> - Virginia

1863: Western Theater

Fall 1862-July 4 - <u>Vicksburg Campaign</u> - Mississippi

May 12 - <u>Battle of Raymond</u> - Mississippi

May 18-July 4 - <u>Siege of Vicksburg</u> - Mississippi

May 16 - <u>Battle of Champion Hill</u> - Mississippi

May 17 - <u>Battle of Big Black River Bridge</u> - Mississippi

May 21-July 9 - <u>Siege of Port Hudson</u> - Louisiana

June 11-July 26 - <u>Morgan's Raid</u> - Tennessee, Kentucky, Indiana, & Ohio

September 18-20 - <u>Battle of Chickamauga</u> - Georgia

November 23-25 - <u>Battle of Chattanooga</u> - Tennessee

November-December - <u>Knoxville Campaign</u> - Tennessee

1864: Trans-Mississippi Theater

January 9-11 - <u>Battle of Arkansas Post</u> - Arkansas

1864: Eastern Theater

February 16 - <u>Submarine *H.L. Hunley* Sinks USS *Housatonic*</u> - South Carolina

February 20 - <u>Battle of Olustee</u> - Florida

May 5-7 - <u>Battle of the Wilderness</u> - Virginia

May 8-21 - <u>Battle of Spotsylvania Court House</u> - Virginia

May 11 - <u>Battle of Yellow Tavern</u> - Virginia

May 16 - <u>Battle of New Market</u> - Virginia

May 23-26 - <u>Battle of North Anna</u> - Virginia

May 31-June 12 - <u>Battle of Cold Harbor</u> - Virginia

June 5 - <u>Battle of Piedmont</u> - Virginia

June 9, 1864-April 2, 1865 - <u>Siege of Petersburg</u> - Virginia

June 11-12 - <u>Battle of Trevilian Station</u> - Virginia

June 21-23 - <u>Battle of Jerusalem Plank Road</u> - Virginia

July 9 - <u>Battle of Monocacy</u> - Maryland

July 24 - <u>Second Battle of Kernstown</u> - Virginia

July 30 - <u>Battle of the Crater</u> - Virginia

August 18-21 - <u>Battle of Globe Tavern</u> - Virginia

September 19 - <u>Third Battle of Winchester (Opequon)</u> - Virginia

September 21-22 - <u>Battle of Fisher's Hill</u> - Virginia

October 2 - <u>Battle of Peebles Farm</u> - Virginia

October 19 - <u>Battle of Cedar Creek</u> - Virginia

October 27-28 - <u>Battle of Boydton Plank Road</u> - Virginia

1864: Western Theater

May 13-15 - <u>Battle of Resaca</u> - Georgia

June 10 - <u>Battle of Brice's Cross Roads</u> - Mississippi

June 27 - <u>Battle of Kennesaw Mountain</u> - Georgia

July 20 - <u>Battle of Peachtree Creek</u> - Georgia

July 22 - <u>Battle of Atlanta</u> - Georgia

July 28 - <u>Battle of Ezra Church</u> - Georgia

August 5 - <u>Battle of Mobile Bay</u> - Alabama

August 31-September 1 - <u>Battle of Jonesboro (Jonesborough)</u> - Georgia

November 15-December 22 - <u>Sherman's March to the Sea</u> - Georgia

November 29 - Battle of Spring Hill - Tennessee

November 30 - Battle of Franklin - Tennessee

December 15-16 - Battle of Nashville - Tennessee

1865: Trans-Mississippi

April 8 - Battle of Mansfield - Louisiana

October 23 - Battle of Westport - Missouri

1865: Eastern Theater

January 13-15 - Second Battle of Fort Fisher - North Carolina

March 25 - Battle of Fort Stedman - Virginia

April 1 - Battle of Five Forks - Virginia

April 6 - Battle of Sayler's Creek (Sailor's Creek) - Virginia

April 9 - Surrender at Appomattox Court House - Virginia

1865: Western Theater

March 19-21 - Battle of Bentonville - North Carolina

Civil War Trivia…

*It is believed that up to 500 women fought disguised as men.

*Mercury and chloroform were used as part of medical treatment.

*Soldiers on both sides marched an average of 15 to 20 miles a day.

 **Five Important Dates of the Civil War:**

1. (1860) The first state, South Carolina, seceded from Union.
2. (1861) The first skirmish, First Battle of Bull Run, occurred.
3. (1863) Congress created the Draft. Every man must serve or find a suitable substitute or pay a $300 fine.
4. (1865) Lee (The Confederacy) surrendered at Appomattox.
5. (1865) 13th Amendment was ratified, thus abolishing slavery.

 **About the American Revolutionary War
(April 19, 1775 – September 3, 1783)**

With the exception of the Civil War, no war has been fought on American soil with greater consequences than the American Revolutionary War, which was also known as the American War of Independence and the Revolutionary War. Here are some important facts pertaining to this war:

*Thirteen American colonies fought for independence from British rule.

*Lots of things led to this war, but the five biggest reasons were the Sugar Act, Stamp Act, Townshend Acts, Boston Massacre, and the Boston Tea Party.

*The Continental Army was led by Commander-in-Chief, George Washington.

*We wanted our independence because Britain forced us to pay high taxes yet gave us no say in how things were done. We had no representation in British Parliament, which led to our battle slogan, "No taxation without representation."

*The war began on April 19, 1775 in Lexington, Massachusetts.

*Our first major victory of this war was the Battle of Saratoga, which is widely believed to have been the turning point in this war.

*The Treaty of Paris was signed in 1783 whereby Britain finally recognized America's independence.

Resources

Fascinating facts about the Civil War can be found at facts.randomhistory.com/civil-war-facts.html

Fun facts about the Revolutionary War can be found on www.revolutionary-war-and-beyond.com/revolutionary-war-facts.html

To find out about special events for any battlefield, such as re-enactments, www.civilwar.org

To find a Military Park, www.nps.gov/findapark/military-remember.htm

One of the most economical ways to visit our parks is to buy an Annual Pass. store.usgs.gov/pass/index.html.

Adults can buy an annual pass that is valid for one full year and authorizes access to all national parks and federal recreation sites. It is good for up to three adult passengers and all children under the age of 16. You must be in a non-commercial vehicle. Seniors (62+) can buy a lifetime pass for a nominal fee. Passes are FREE for US Military (and dependents), volunteers, and the disabled (Access Pass). Applicants must have a valid ID or proper documentation.

TERRANCE ZEPKE
Series Reading Order
& Guide

Series List

Most Haunted Series

Terrance Talks Travel Series

Cheap Travel Series

Spookiest Series

Stop Talking Series

Carolinas for Kids Series

Ghosts of the Carolinas Series

Books & Guides for the Carolinas Series

& More Books by Terrance Zepke

≈

Introduction

Here is a list of titles by Terrance Zepke. They are presented in chronological order although they do not need to be read in any particular order.

Also included is an author bio, a personal message from Terrance, and some other information you may find helpful.

All books are available as digital and print books. They can be found on Amazon, Barnes and Noble, Kobo, Apple iBooks, GooglePlay, Smashwords, or through your favorite independent bookseller.

For more about this author and her books visit her Author Page at:

http://www.amazon.com/Terrance-Zepke/e/B000APJNIA/.

You can also connect with Terrance on Twitter **@terrancezepke** or on

www.facebook.com/terrancezepke

www.pinterest.com/terrancezepke

www.goodreads.com/terrancezepke

Sign up for weekly email notifications of the *Terrance Talks Travel* blog to be the first to learn about new episodes of her travel show, cheap travel tips, free downloadable TRAVEL REPORTS, and discover her TRIP PICK OF THE WEEK at www.terrancetalkstravel.com or sign up for her *Mostly Ghostly* blog at www.terrancezepke.com.

≈

You can follow her travel show, **TERRANCE TALKS TRAVEL: ÜBER ADVENTURES on www.blogtalkradio.com/terrancetalkstravel** or subscribe to it at **iTunes.**

Warning: Listening to this show could lead to a spectacular South African safari, hot-air ballooning over the Swiss Alps, Disney Adventures, and Tornado Tours!

≈

Terrance Zepke is co-host of the writing show, **A WRITER'S JOURNEY: FROM BLANK PAGE TO PUBLISHED.** All episodes can be found on **iTunes** or on **www.terrancezepke.com.**

≈

AUTHOR BIO

Terrance Zepke studied Journalism at the University of Tennessee and later received a Master's degree in Mass Communications from the University of South Carolina. She studied parapsychology at the renowned Rhine Research Center.

Zepke spends much of her time happily traveling around the world but always returns home to the Carolinas where she lives part-time in both states. She has written hundreds of articles and more than fifty books. She is the host of *Terrance Talks Travel: Über Adventures* and co-host of *A Writer's Journey: From Blank Page to Published*. Additionally, this award-winning and best-selling author has been featured in many publications and programs, such as NPR, CNN, *The Washington Post,* Associated Press, Travel with Rick Steves, Around the World, *Publishers Weekly,* World Travel & Dining with Pierre Wolfe, *San Francisco Chronicle*, Good Morning Show, *Detroit Free Press*, The Learning Channel, and The Travel Channel.

When she's not investigating haunted places, searching for pirate treasure, or climbing lighthouses, she is most likely packing for her next adventure to some far flung place, such as Reykjavik or Kwazulu Natal. Some of her favorite adventures include piranha fishing on the Amazon, shark cage diving in South Africa, hiking the Andes Mountains Inca Trail, camping in the Himalayas, dog-sledding in the Arctic Circle, and a gorilla safari in the Congo.

≈

MOST HAUNTED SERIES

A Ghost Hunter's Guide to the Most Haunted Places in America
(2012)
https://read.amazon.com/kp/embed?asin=B0085SG22O&previe
w=newtab&linkCode=kpe&ref_=cm_sw_r_kb_dp_zerQwb1AM
J0R4

A Ghost Hunter's Guide to the Most Haunted Houses in America
(2013)
https://read.amazon.com/kp/embed?asin=B00C3PUMGC&previ
ew=newtab&linkCode=kpe&ref_=cm_sw_r_kb_dp_BfrQwb1W
F1Y6T

*A Ghost Hunter's Guide to the Most Haunted Hotels & Inns in
America* (2014)
https://read.amazon.com/kp/embed?asin=B00C3PUMGC&previ
ew=newtab&linkCode=kpe

*A Ghost Hunter's Guide to the Most Haunted Historic Sites in
America* (2016)
https://www.amazon.com/Ghost-Hunters-Haunted-Historic-
America-
ebook/dp/B01LXADK90/ref=sr_1_1?s=books&ie=UTF8&qid=1
475973918&sr=1-
1&keywords=a+ghost+hunter%27s+guide+to+the+most+haunte
d+historic+sites+in+america

*The Ghost Hunter's MOST HAUNTED Box Set (3 in 1):
Discover America's Most Haunted Destinations* (2016)
https://read.amazon.com/kp/embed?asin=B01HISAAJM&previe
w=newtab&linkCode=kpe&ref_=cm_sw_r_kb_dp_ulz-
xbNKND7VT

MOST HAUNTED and SPOOKIEST Sampler Box Set: Featuring *A GHOST HUNTER'S GUIDE TO THE MOST HAUNTED PLACES IN AMERICA* and *SPOOKIEST CEMETERIES* (2017)

https://read.amazon.com/kp/embed?asin=B01N17EEOM&preview=newtab&linkCode=kpe&ref_=cm_sw_r_kb_dp_.JFLybCTN3QEF

≈

TERRANCE TALKS TRAVEL SERIES

Terrance Talks Travel: A Pocket Guide to South Africa (2015)
https://read.amazon.com/kp/embed?asin=B00PSTFTLI&preview
=newtab&linkCode=kpe&ref_=cm_sw_r_kb_dp_pirQwb12XZX
65

Terrance Talks Travel: A Pocket Guide to African Safaris (2015)
https://read.amazon.com/kp/embed?asin=B00PSTFZSA&previe
w=newtab&linkCode=kpe&ref_=cm_sw_r_kb_dp_jhrQwb0P8Z
87G

Terrance Talks Travel: A Pocket Guide to Adventure Travel
(2015)
https://read.amazon.com/kp/embed?asin=B00UKMAVQG&prev
iew=newtab&linkCode=kpe&ref_=cm_sw_r_kb_dp_ThrQwb1P
VVZAZ

Terrance Talks Travel: A Pocket Guide to Florida Keys
(including Key West & The Everglades) (2016)
http://www.amazon.com/Terrance-Talks-Travel-Including-
Everglades-
ebook/dp/B01EWHML58/ref=sr_1_1?s=books&ie=UTF8&qid=
1461897775&sr=1-
1&keywords=terrance+talks+travel%3A+a+pocket+guide+to+th
e+florida+keys

Terrance Talks Travel: The Quirky Tourist Guide to Key West
(2017)
https://www.amazon.com/Terrance-
Zepke/e/B000APJNIA/ref=sr_ntt_srch_lnk_1?qid=1485052308
&sr=8-1

Terrance Talks Travel: The Quirky Tourist Guide to Cape Town
(2017)
https://www.amazon.com/Terrance-

Zepke/e/B000APJNIA/ref=sr_ntt_srch_lnk_1?qid=1485052308&sr=8-1

Terrance Talks Travel: The Quirky Tourist Guide to Reykjavik (2017)
https://www.amazon.com/Terrance-Zepke/e/B000APJNIA/ref=sr_ntt_srch_lnk_15?qid=1488514258&sr=8-15

Terrance Talks Travel: The Quirky Tourist Guide to Charleston, South Carolina (2017)
https://www.amazon.com/Terrance-Zepke/e/B000APJNIA/ref=sr_ntt_srch_lnk_15?qid=1488514258&sr=8-15

Terrance Talks Travel: The Quirky Tourist Guide to Ushuaia (2017)
https://www.amazon.com/Terrance-Zepke/e/B000APJNIA/ref=sr_ntt_srch_lnk_15?qid=1488514258&sr=8-15

Terrance Talks Travel: The Quirky Tourist Guide to Antarctica (2017) https://www.amazon.com/Terrance-Zepke/e/B000APJNIA/ref=sr_ntt_srch_lnk_1?qid=1489092624&sr=8-1

TERRANCE TALKS TRAVEL: The Quirky Tourist Guide to Machu Picchu & Cuzco (Peru) 2017
https://read.amazon.com/kp/embed?asin=B07147HLQY&preview=newtab&linkCode=kpe&ref_=cm_sw_r_kb_dp_HmZmzb9FT5E0P

African Safari Box Set: Featuring TERRANCE TALKS TRAVEL: *A Pocket Guide to South Africa* and *TERRANCE TALKS TRAVEL: A Pocket Guide to African Safaris* (2017)
https://read.amazon.com/kp/embed?asin=B01MUH6VJU&preview=newtab&linkCode=kpe&ref_=cm_sw_r_kb_dp_xLFLybAQKFA0B

≈

Terrance Zepke

CHEAP TRAVEL SERIES

How to Cruise Cheap! (2017)

https://www.amazon.com/Cruise-Cheap-CHEAP-TRAVEL-Book-ebook/dp/B01N6NYM1N/

How to Fly Cheap! (2017)

https://www.amazon.com/How-Cheap-CHEAP-TRAVEL-Book-ebook/dp/B01N7Q81YG/

How to Travel Cheap! (2017)

https://read.amazon.com/kp/embed?asin=B01N7Q81YG&preview=newtab&linkCode=kpe&ref_=cm_sw_r_kb_dp_j78KybJVSCXDX

How to Travel FREE or Get Paid to Travel! (2017)

https://read.amazon.com/kp/embed?asin=B01N7Q81YG&preview=newtab&linkCode=kpe&ref_=cm_sw_r_kb_dp_j78KybJVSCXDX

CHEAP TRAVEL SERIES (4 IN 1) BOX SET (2017)

https://read.amazon.com/kp/embed?asin=B071ZGV1TY&preview=newtab&linkCode=kpe&ref_=cm_sw_r_kb_dp_rlZmzbSPV8KG9

SPOOKIEST SERIES

Spookiest Lighthouses (2013)
https://read.amazon.com/kp/embed?asin=B00EAAQA2S&preview

Spookiest Battlefields (2015)
https://read.amazon.com/kp/embed?asin=B00XUSWS3G&preview=newtab&linkCode=kpe&ref_=cm_sw_r_kb_dp_okrQwb0TR9F8M

Spookiest Cemeteries (2016)
http://www.amazon.com/Terrance-Zepke/e/B000APJNIA/ref=sr_ntt_srch_lnk_1?qid=1457641303&sr=8-1

Spookiest Objects (2017)
https://read.amazon.com/kp/embed?asin=B0728FMVZF&preview=newtab&linkCode=kpe&ref_=cm_sw_r_kb_dp_eqZmzbN2172VR

Spookiest Box Set (3 in 1): Discover America's Most Haunted Destinations (2016)
https://read.amazon.com/kp/embed?asin=B01HH2OM4I&preview=newtab&linkCode=kpe&ref_=cm_sw_r_kb_dp_Anz-xbT3SDEZS

MOST HAUNTED and SPOOKIEST Sampler Box Set: Featuring *A GHOST HUNTER'S GUIDE TO THE MOST HAUNTED PLACES IN AMERICA* and *SPOOKIEST CEMETERIES* (2017)

https://read.amazon.com/kp/embed?asin=B01N17EEOM&preview=newtab&linkCode=kpe&ref_=cm_sw_r_kb_dp_.JFLybCTN3QEF

≈

STOP TALKING SERIES

Stop Talking & Start Writing Your Book (2015)
https://read.amazon.com/kp/embed?asin=B012YHTIAY&previe
w=newtab&linkCode=kpe&ref_=cm_sw_r_kb_dp_qlrQwb1N7G
3YF

Stop Talking & Start Publishing Your Book (2015)
https://read.amazon.com/kp/embed?asin=B013HHV1LE&previe
w=newtab&linkCode=kpe&ref_=cm_sw_r_kb_dp_WlrQwb1F6
3MFD

Stop Talking & Start Selling Your Book (2015)
https://read.amazon.com/kp/embed?asin=B015YAO33K&previe
w=newtab&linkCode=kpe&ref_=cm_sw_r_kb_dp_ZkrQwb188J
8BE

Stop Talking & Start Writing Your Book Series (3 in 1) Box Set
(2016) https://www.amazon.com/Stop-Talking-Start-Writing-
Box-
ebook/dp/B01M58J5AZ/ref=sr_1_5?s=books&ie=UTF8&qid=1
475974073&sr=1-5&keywords=stop+talking+and+start+writing

≈

CAROLINAS FOR KIDS SERIES

Lighthouses of the Carolinas for Kids (2009)
http://www.amazon.com/Lighthouses-Carolinas-Kids-Terrance-Zepke/dp/1561644293/ref=asap_bc?ie=UTF8

Pirates of the Carolinas for Kids (2009)
https://read.amazon.com/kp/embed?asin=B01BJ3VSWK&preview=newtab&linkCode=kpe&ref_=cm_sw_r_kb_dp_rGrXwb0XDTSTA

Ghosts of the Carolinas for Kids (2011)
https://read.amazon.com/kp/embed?asin=B01BJ3VSVQ&preview=newtab&linkCode=kpe&ref_=cm_sw_r_kb_dp_XLrXwb0E7N1AK

≈

GHOSTS OF THE CAROLINAS SERIES

Ghosts of the Carolina Coasts (1999)
http://www.amazon.com/Ghosts-Carolina-Coasts-Terrance-Zepke/dp/1561641758/ref=asap_bc?ie=UTF8

The Best Ghost Tales of South Carolina (2004)
http://www.amazon.com/Best-Ghost-Tales-South-Carolina/dp/1561643068/ref=asap_bc?ie=UTF8

Ghosts & Legends of the Carolina Coasts (2005)
https://read.amazon.com/kp/embed?asin=B01AGQJABW&preview=newtab&linkCode=kpe&ref_=cm_sw_r_kb_dp_VKrXwb1Q09794

The Best Ghost Tales of North Carolina (2006)
https://read.amazon.com/kp/embed?asin=B01BJ3VSV6&preview=newtab&linkCode=kpe&ref_=cm_sw_r_kb_dp_6IrXwb0XKT90Q

≈

BOOKS & GUIDES FOR THE CAROLINAS SERIES

Pirates of the Carolinas (2005)
http://www.amazon.com/Pirates-Carolinas-Terrance-Zepke/dp/1561643440/ref=asap_bc?ie=UTF8

Coastal South Carolina: Welcome to the Lowcountry (2006)
http://www.amazon.com/Coastal-South-Carolina-Welcome-Lowcountry/dp/1561643483/ref=asap_bc?ie=UTF8

Coastal North Carolina: Its Enchanting Islands, Towns & Communities (2011)
http://www.amazon.com/Coastal-North-Carolina-Terrance-Zepke/dp/1561645117/ref=asap_bc?ie=UTF8

Lighthouses of the Carolinas: A Short History & Guide (2011)
https://read.amazon.com/kp/embed?asin=B01AGQJA7G&preview=newtab&linkCode=kpe&ref_=cm_sw_r_kb_dp_UHrXwb09A22P1

≈

MORE BOOKS BY TERRANCE ZEPKE

Lowcountry Voodoo: Tales, Spells & Boo Hags (2009)
https://read.amazon.com/kp/embed?asin=B018WAGUC6&previ
ew=newtab&linkCode=kpe&ref_=cm_sw_r_kb_dp_UmrQwb19
AVSYG

Ghosts of Savannah (2012)
http://www.amazon.com/Ghosts-Savannah-Terrance-
Zepke/dp/1561645303/ref=asap_bc?ie=UTF8

How to Train Any Puppy or Dog Using Three Simple Strategies
(2017)
https://www.amazon.com/Train-Puppy-Using-Simple-Strategies-
ebook/dp/B01MZ5GN2M/ref=asap_bc?ie=UTF8

*Fiction books written under a pseudonym

≈

Message from the Author

The primary purpose of this guide is to introduce you to some titles you may not have known about. Another reason for it is to let you know all the ways you can connect with me. Authors love to hear from readers. We truly appreciate you more than you'll ever know. Please feel free to send me a comment or question via the comment form found on every page on www.terrancezepke.com and www.terrancetalkstravel.com or follow me on your favorite social media. Don't forget that you can also listen to my writing podcast on iTunes, **A Writer's Journey**, or my travel show, **Terrance Talks Travel: Über Adventures** on Blog Talk Radio and iTunes. The best way to make sure you don't miss any episodes of these shows (and find a complete archive of shows), new book releases and giveaways, contests, my TRIP PICK OF THE WEEK, cheap travel tips, free downloadable ghost and travel reports, and more is to subscribe to *Terrance Talks Travel* on www.terrancetalkstravel.com or ***Mostly Ghostly*** on www.terrancezepke.com. If you'd like to learn more about any of my books, you can find in-depth descriptions and "look inside" options through most online booksellers. Also, please note that links to book previews have been included in SERIES section of this booklet for your convenience.

Thank you for your interest and HAPPY READING!

Terrance

See the next page for a sneak peek of

SPOOKIEST LIGHTHOUSES: Discover America's Most Haunted Lighthouses

New London Ledge Lighthouse

Location: New London (harbor), Connecticut

Built: 1909

Visitor Information: OPEN TO THE PUBLIC.

The light is operational but has been automated since 1986. There is no staff at New London Ledge Lighthouse. During the summer months, tours can be arranged through Project Oceanology (www.oceanology.org). This 2.5-hour tour includes time inside the tower. Area ferries and cruise tours offer views of the lighthouse, but this is the only one that permits inside access. The lighthouse, which is on the National Register of Historic Places, is owned by the US Coast Guard and managed by the New London Ledge Lighthouse Foundation.

About the Haunted Lighthouse: Architectural buffs will note the French and Colonial influences that are prevalent in this unusual-looking beacon. It is a combination Victorian mansion and lighthouse. Interestingly, the crib (made of pine, iron, and steel) was built and then transported to this site using four tugboats. Upon arrival at its new home, the crib was filled with concrete, riprap, and gravel and then sunk. A concrete pier was built on top of the crib and the tower placed on top of it. Originally, it had a fourth-order Fresnel lens in the lantern room, which illuminated three white flashes followed by one red flash.

It is reportedly haunted by former keeper John "Ernie" Randolph. When Ernie took the assignment, he brought his second wife with him. His new bride was half his age. They were happy—in the beginning. But as time went on, she grew restless and bored—and unhappy and lonely.

One day while Ernie was out securing supplies, a ferry captain stopped by to check on the couple. The desperate woman threw some belongings in a bag, scribbled a "Dear Ernie" note, and left with the ferry captain. When Ernie returned and read the note from his wife, he became so despondent that he killed himself. That was in 1936.

But it seems that Ernie is still here—and he is a mischievous spirit. He often moves tools and books in the library. He turns the foghorn on. He tidies the place. A keeper's wife, who lived here during the 1940s, saw an apparition she thinks was Ernie. Her husband, who wouldn't admit to believing in ghosts, did admit that possessions he kept safeguarded in a locked desk drawer were often rearranged. The couple also reported an unidentifiable fishy odor and cold spots. Others have reported seeing a shadowy figure on occasion.

When Coast Guard crew members were stationed here, they reported knocking on their bedroom doors during the night. The television turned on and off seemingly on its own. Doors often open and close. Floors and windows have been meticulously cleaned, but no one knows by whom. None of the staff takes credit when asked who did the nice job on the windows. But perhaps the spookiest thing was when the covers were pulled off the bed of Coast Guard crew members by an unseen presence. The men admitted they had trouble getting back to sleep after seeing their blankets removed by a ghost. The lighthouse has been featured on the television shows, *Scariest Places on Earth* and *Ghost Hunters*.

Index